Naming Your Business and Its Products and Services *

*How to Create Effective Trade Names, Trademarks, and Service Marks to Attract Customers, Protect Your Goodwill and Reputation, and Stay Out of Court!

Phillip G. Williams

Small Business Bookshelf Series
Volume 2

The P. Gaines Co.
PO Box 2253, Oak Park, Illinois 60303

Since laws are subject to differing interpretations, neither the publisher nor the author offers any guarantees concerning the information contained in this publication or the use to which it is put. Although this publication is designed to provide accurate and authoritative information concerning trade names, trademarks, and service marks, it is sold with the understanding that neither the author nor the publisher is engaged in rendering legal or other professional advice. If legal or other expert assistance is required, the services of a competent professional should be sought. *Adapted from a Declaration of Principles jointly adopted by a Committee of the American Bar Association and a Committee of Publishers.*

Permission is gratefully acknowledged to reprint illustrations from the following publications:
Pictorial Archive of Quaint Woodcuts in the Chap Book Style by Joseph Crawhall, selected and arranged by Theodore Menten (New York: Dover Publications, 1974).
Old-Fashioned Animal Cuts, edited by Carol Belanger Grafton (New York: Dover Publications, 1987).
Old-Fashioned Mortised Cuts, edited by Carol Belanger Grafton (New York: Dover Publications, 1987).
Old-Fashioned Patriotic Cuts, edited by Carol Belanger Grafton (New York: Dover Publications, 1988).
Old-Fashioned Romantic Cuts, edited by Carol Belanger Grafton (New York: Dover Publications, 1987).
Pictorial Archive of Printer's Ornaments from the Renaissance to the 20th Century, selected by Carol Belanger Grafton (New York: Dover Publications, 1980).
Fanciful Victorian Initials, edited by Carol Belanger Grafton (New York: Dover Publications, 1984).
Old-Fashioned Transportation Cuts, edited by Carol Belanger Grafton (New York: Dover Publications, 1987).
Ready-To-Use Decorative Letters, edited by Carol Belanger Grafton (New York: Dover Publications, 1986).

Library of Congress Cataloging in Publication Data

Williams, Phil, 1946-
    Naming your business and its products and services : how to create
effective trade names, trademarks, and service marks to attract
customers, protect your goodwill and reputation, and stay out of
court / Phillip G. Williams.
        p.   cm. -- (Small business bookshelf series : v. 2)
    Includes bibliographical references and index.
    ISBN 0-936284-10-2 (paper : acid-free) : $19.95
    1. Trademarks--United States--Popular works. 2. Business names-
-United States--Popular works.   I. Title. II. Series.
KF3180.Z9W54 1990
346.7304'88--dc20   90-3434
[347.306488]   CIP

Manufactured in the United States of America.

Table of Contents

"A good name is better than great riches."—
Cervantes's <u>Don Quixote</u>

What are com-mercial names?

There exist three broad classes of names used in commerce: trade names, trademarks, and service marks.

The trade name

The name which designates a business—whether a sole proprietorship, a partnership, or a corporation—such as FORD MOTOR COMPANY, is called a ***trade name.***

The trademark

The brand names which designate a company's products, whether they are cars, cookies, or cassocks (for example, CAMERO, OREO, BEAUVEST), is termed a ***trademark.***

The service mark

The name which designates the services that a business provides the public, for instance, HYATT LEGAL SERVICES or MR. GOODWRENCH, is called a ***service mark.***

Design elements

Trade names, trademarks, and service marks may all employ designs as well as words (such as ELSIE THE COW, THREE RED CARNATIONS, or THE SHELL of SHELL OIL CO.) as part of the identity of a particular company, its products, or its services. While designs are an important area in their own right, this book will focus on the verbal element of marks, the *words* that are used as names in commerce. Many companies, such as KELLOGG'S, AVON, and XEROX, rely *only* on a name (rendered in a distinctive graphic style) to serve as the carrier of their unique commercial identity. Other businesses, from DU PONT (the name appearing inside an oval) to LEVI'S (symbolized by a logo with a jeans patch pocket) and MCDONALD'S (denoted by golden arches), have adopted some form of pictorial element as an integral part of their corporate personality. A trademark can also consist of a name, logo, *and* slogan, as in the case of MAXWELL HOUSE coffee, pictured with a tilted cup of coffee and the words, "Good to the last drop."

If you are interested in creating a logo as a part of your business trade name, trademark, or service mark, we highly recommend an excellent book on this topic, *How to Design Trade Marks and Logos* by John Murphy and Michael Rowe.

Every business needs a name

Every company, from the smallest sole proprietorship to the largest multinational corporation, has to have a trade name. Every business, therefore, must deal with the selection of a name on at least this one level. In addition, many businesses will need to construct either a brand name (trademark) or a service mark at some point. Businesses that manufacture goods *and* offer services to the public, furthermore, will have need of all three classes of names: in addition to their trade name, they will possess one or more trademarks and one or more service marks.

In a small business that provides one service only, say lawn care, the trade name and the service mark will generally be the same. In other words, the company name will function as the brand name of the particular service provided by the business. For this reason, small service industries should choose their company names with special care.

Martha, do you prefer "George" or "Moon Unit"?

Every business, then, will be involved in the selection of a name, whether for one, two, or all three of these classes of commercial names. Many business owners name their business—or their products or services—like they name their children. While you cannot normally be sued for whatever moniker you inflict on your child, this is clearly *not* the case with commercial names. Not only will you be liable for damages in trademark infringement cases. You can, in addition, be forced to give up an ill-chosen name and thus lose the reputation and goodwill that you have built around it, through advertising, promotion and conscientious service.

The world of business names and naming is one fraught with problems, pitfalls, and potential disaster for the unwary. A well-crafted name, chosen with an eye to artistry as well as legal considerations, on the other hand, becomes a very valuable business asset, which, in the case of successful companies, may come to be worth literally millions of dollars. Choose your name wisely, therefore; the more forceful your selection in terms of its power to communicate, the more effective your product or service will prove itself to be in the marketplace.

Large companies may spend many thousands of dollars on developing a commercial name and having it searched for legal clearance. There exist businesses that specialize solely in name development for other businesses, just as there are attorneys whose practice centers on the searching of trade names, trademarks, and service marks to determine their legality. Smaller companies may not

12

have the financial resources available for these kinds of customized professional name services, however. Fees may run as high as $150,000 nowadays for the creation of a corporate identity. This book is designed to provide the small business owner-operator with basic guidelines on the major legal and aesthetic issues involved in name selection, since the same dangers that may befall a large business may as easily befall a small one in the realm of trademark practice.

All names used in commerce should be chosen with extreme care, for two reasons: First, the effectiveness (or ineffectiveness) of the name may be decisive to the success or failure of the business. Second, the adoption of a commercial name already being used by another business may *in itself* result in an infringement lawsuit against the Johnny-come-lately who has unknowingly taken over someone else's name as his own. *All* businesses, whether corporations or sole proprietorships or partnerships, are subject equally to the commercial and legal risks which a poor name choice involves. Conversely, each form of business will also stand to share in the rewards which a memorable, effective, legally defendable name produces.

Some Statistics

❑ Almost a million businesses are started in the United States each year—Every one of these new enterprises needs a company trade name.

❑ The federal Patent and Trademark Office (PTO) registered its first trademarks in the year 1881.

❑ Over 50,000 new products come to market each year in the United States, each requiring a brand name.

❑ The oldest trademark still in use in the United States is that of the SAMSON CORDAGE WORKS OF BOSTON; its logo is based on the biblical theme of Samson wrestling a lion.

❑ Some 70,000 new trademarks are currently registered each year with the PTO.

❑ Worldwide, approximately 750,000 trademarks are registered each year.

❑ The PTO issued its one millionth trademark registration on December 17, 1974.

❑ There presently are some 20 million registered trademarks worldwide.

The purpose of trademarks, trade names, and service marks

What is in a name? That which we call a rose by any other name would smell as sweet. Or so imagines Juliet about her beloved Romeo in Shakespeare's famous play. The decisive role which names often play in our world seems to suggest otherwise, however. From the oatmeal you eat for breakfast to the car you drive and the stockings you wear, you rely upon commercial names to communicate vital information about virtually every aspect of your life. This power of commercial names to communicate, furthermore, is directly tied to their economic worth. In the business realm, we see that particular names may nowadays come to be valued at literally millions of dollars on the corporate balance sheet. When one publicly traded company buys another, what is often being purchased is primarily nothing more than brand names, whose value has been built up over the years to sometimes astronomical levels. THE COCA-COLA CO., for example, currently values its brand names at over $1 billion. This worth attached to brand names affects the consumer's perception of the worth of products as well. To take an extreme example, a watch carrying the CARTIER mark will command a much higher price than one named Shapiro or Williams!

The trademark plays a role for us comparable to that of the totemic animal for a primitive tribe. The name and image of the animal which a tribe selects as its totem provide an emotional rallying point around which the identity of the tribe forms, embodying tradition and engendering loyalty. Similarly, rival sports teams today have their own "totemic" figures, such as mascots, and their own identifying colors, songs, and even legends. Likewise, rival companies who are competing for market share—often with similar or even the same products—invest their trademarks

15

in a comparable way with their own associations and their own mythologies and ideals, conveyed to the public through advertising. The commercial mark serves, then, as a means of focus; through it, a company gives a product a distinctive personality of its own and thus distinguishes its products from that of others.

Think of how many different brands of detergent you can buy today, with names like TIDE, OXYDOL, CHEER, or how many different kinds of cars are available under various nomenclatures, from ESCORT to MERCEDES-BENZ. While some of these trademarks denote products that are virtually identical, although sold under different names, others stand for truly unique goods or services. But, in each case, the trademark provides a tangible symbol for the consumer, with its own unique associations.

The common denominator underlying all such marks in use in commerce is that each points the buyer to a unique source of supply, whether appearing on an article of merchandise to identify the manufacturer, or in connection with a service, such as insurance or communications or day care, to identify the provider, or, in the instance of a profit or nonprofit business or other entity, to identify the organization itself.

The commercial name not only identifies the product or service or organization and distinguishes it from all others but also provides vital information regarding the quality of the goods or services offered. The most appropriate and effective names, furthermore, not only distinguish and personalize but also trigger consumer desire. The commercial name can take on a life of its own, becoming, under the right circumstances, a valuable asset in its own right, legally defendable and marketable, with the evaluation of the worth of the name itself in the case of the sale of the business or the franchising or merchandising of the name as a separate commodity.

The name as measure of your aspirations

If your highest goal in life is merely to get by by hook or crook, without any commitment to reach your highest potential, you will probably settle for most any name for your business. Such an approach destines you to remain small. Even if you call yourself McDonalds Hot Dogs or A&P Submarines, chances are that MCDONALD'S or the GREAT ATLANTIC AND PACIFIC TEA COMPANY will never hear of you, to haul you into court. But if you plan to be a force in the business world to be reckoned with, let your choice of a name convey the height of your aspirations, the depth of your commitment. Seek a name which reflects your own unique sense of identity.

A mackerel by any other name . . .

What is in a name? Ideally, everything. Not every name, of course, communicates the essence of the reality it stands for, although we unconsciously long for such a world in which the name and the thing are identical. The most astute marketing techniques recognize the almost magical quality of names to conjure up a reality. Unless your potential audience is that of prepubescent punk rocker wanabees, you would not dub your plush toy dog "Vicious" any more than you would buy a bread named "Stale." In the business world, the best names often, although not always, promise

17

something desirable: pleasure, profit, convenience, self-confidence, comfort, affection. In some buying sectors, of course, there is a reverse chic operating, which makes light of the very values that the general populace holds dear. In these terrains, the same rules hold, except that *all* values are reversed.

Pain is exalted over pleasure, hate over love, and so on. Thirteen-year-old boys, the very affluent, and the jaded, for instance, may all deviate from the usual pattern of response to names that promise conventional rewards. The watchword is, get to know intimately the desires of your targeted buyers and let the name match the mental profile of this group.

The selection of a suitable and effective name for your business is one of the most important decisions you will make. For your name is your "calling card" which communicates to others what you want them to know about your company. An attractive, thoughtful name will attract customers, just as a drab, lifeless name will repel them. You will have to back up the promise which your name makes about you, of course. The best of names, if unsupported by solid achievement, will draw customers but cannot keep them for long, once they learn that the sandwich or the satellite does not live up to the expectations raised. In that case, your "good" name will quickly become a liability, becoming identified in the public's view with that which is inflated, deceptive, and false.

Your name can play a valuable role for you, the business owner, as well as for the customer. If your name sets a high standard of precision of thought and action, it will serve as a constant reminder, to you as well as to others, of the lofty goals upon which your business is based. The name which falls flat on the ear and the mind, by contrast, is a constant reminder of the absence of any such goals or standards. A mediocre name will tend to mire you in mediocrity, unless, of course, you transcend the infelicitous name which you have been saddled with and select a new name which better communicates the *quality* of your work.

Even large companies change their names in the course of time to reflect a new sense of vision and purpose. One well-known case is that of CONSOLIDATED FOODS. Within a year after altering its name to SARA LEE, the stock of the company doubled in value. This dramatically increased valuation by the marketplace was directly tied to its corporate identity change, reflected by its new name. Certain critics of this particular name change pointed out that the new name did not provide any more information about the other aspects of the business, besides food, than the old one did. Nevertheless, the new name is clearly an improvement. ☆☆☆☆**SARA LEE**☆☆☆☆ has personality; **CONSOLIDATED FOODS** is abstract and stodgy.

In a recent two-page ad

in the *Wall Street Journal*, captioned "Some Names Just Communicate Better Than Others," the HARRIS 3/M COMPANY announced its company trade name change to LANIER. The ad goes on to note other famous name "changes"—William Henry Pratt to Boris Karloff, Frances Guinin to Judy Garland, William Claude Dukenfield to W.C. Fields, and Ernest Evans to Chubby Checker!

Once you have recognized

the value of a good business name, what steps do you need to take to come up with an appropriate identifier for your company, whether you are naming a new business or renaming an old one? How do you go about finding a name or names for your product(s) and/or services?

Business names have been arrived at in almost every conceivable fashion, from the case of the man looking for a name for his cigars when a white owl flew in his window (WHITE OWL cigars), to the instance of a name suggested from a Bible reading in church (IVORY soap, from Psalm 45), to the name for a cleanser originally designed to appeal to the ethnic nature of its main buyers, French-Canadian housewives (BON AMI cleanser). There is no one procedure for producing the right business name. The one common denominator of all successful name searches, even those completed through chance or whim, is an intimate knowledge of the market of a particular business and the nature of its products or services. Without this knowledge, you won't recognize a good name even if it flies right in your face.

We will plunge headfirst

into some of the main legal issues of business names, then consider the art and science of naming. This is the reverse order from that which those searching for a name will follow. The usual approach is **first** to come up with a potential name or names considered best expressive of a business or product or service. Only **then** does one consider possible conflicts with already existing names or other legal problems. The astute namesmith, however, will want to be aware from the start of the legal considerations which will automatically eliminate certain types of names and render others of highly questionable value.

Trademark Law 101

Article I, Section 8 of the Constitution of the United States grants Congress the power to establish a system of copyrights as well as a system of patents. Exclusive federal authority over these domains of author and inventor rights and a long history of federal legislation going back to 1790 have resulted in a high degree of order and consistency in these two areas. Trademark law, by contrast, appears downright chaotic. No provision at all is made in the Constitution for trademarks. Consequently, both the federal and state governments have evolved trademark legislation which is overlapping in some areas and inconsistent in others. A thorough knowledge about these problems offers our best defense against them.

Trademarks, copyrights, and patents

T rademarks, copyrights, and patents each protect individual rights of usage but in distinct ways. The domain of trademark protection is much less clearly defined and more open to interpretation than the other two. Whereas a patent protects one's rights to an invention and a copyright guards one's rights to written or musical works generally, a trademark (or service mark) is designed to protect its owner from unfair usage of the same mark, or a confusingly similar one, by another party. The ways in which this purpose is interpreted by the U.S. Patent and Trademark Office, according to certain rules, guidelines, and exceptions, will be considered hereafter.

Our legal system in this country, derived from the British common law model, grounds the exclusive right to use a recognizably distinct trade name, trademark or service mark in the name's *first* and *continued* use in commerce. All those countries, including the United States, which base their legal systems on the Common Law of England have *optional* trademark registration systems designed to protect against infringers. Registration per se conveys no ownership rights; first usage of the name in commerce alone determines the rightful owner of the mark.

One other major difference between trademarks and copyrights and patents: trademarks can be renewed indefinitely (see page 25), whereas both copyrights and patents have a limited life and expire after a set number of years.

21

Federal v. state trademark law

Interstate and intrastate commerce

In general, the amended federal Trademark Act of 1946 (often referred to as the Lanham Act) governs commerce with foreign nations and interstate commerce (commerce between states), while individual state laws govern intrastate commerce (commerce within a particular state's borders).

Registration

Both the federal and state governments provide an optional registry for trademarks and service marks. If your mark is used *only* in intrastate commerce, however, it may be registered on the state level solely, *not* on the federal register. If it is used in interstate commerce, it may be registered on both the state and federal registries.

Many states do not register service marks, so that there exists no clearcut way to determine if a particular mark in a given state is already in use or not. Needless to say, this leads to confusion. The search techniques discussed in Part 3 of this book offer your best means of discovery of unregistered marks in current usage.

This book covers the main points of federal trademark law. The trademark legislation of many states follows closely that of the federal government. To find out about the laws governing trademarks in your individual state, request a copy of the trademark statutes and an application form to register a trademark from your state government. Most states have an Office of the Secretary of State or a Division of Commerce which will be able to steer you to the right division for trademark information. Larger public libraries will also have a copy of the trademark laws for your state. A publication put out by the United States Trademark Association, titled *State Trademark and Unfair Competition Law,* presents as well as analyzes trademark laws in each of the fifty states and the District of Columbia. This volume is available at many law libraries.

Overview of use and registration of federal trademarks

Before looking at the ins and outs of selecting a suitable trademark or service mark or trade name, let us consider how the whole process of trademarks works. In the past, the first step to acquiring a federal trademark was putting it into use in interstate (or foreign) commerce. Registration followed therafter. This approach still stands. The Trademark Law Revision Act of 1988, which went into effect November 16, 1989, has created a second registration procedure as well, based on intent to use. An intent-to-use application may now be filed on the basis of a bona fide *intention* to use the mark in commerce for specific goods or services. In such a case, the application is approved by the PTO if it does not appear to be in conflict with other existing marks. It is then published in the trademark section of the *Official Gazette*. If, after publication, no one opposes the mark, the applicant is sent a Notice of Allowance. One then has six months to place the mark into commercial use and file a Declaration of Use; this period can be extended for up to 36 months (but a $100 fee must be paid for each 6-month extension). Both types of application (use-based and intent-to-use) file the same form (See Appendix C, "Trademark/Service Mark Application, Principal Register, with Declaration").

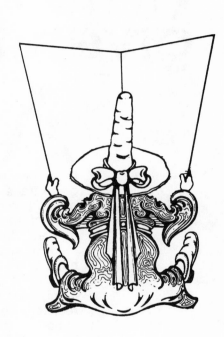

In actual practice, the first step to registering a trademark or service mark under either the use-based application or the intent-to use application should be the conduct of a trademark search. If you then find that someone else is already using the same name to market the same class of goods as that which you have chosen, you should, of course, abandon the name and choose another. Other cases of *similar names* are less clear cut. A similar name for the same class of goods may also have to be abandoned, but the same name for a different class of goods will be allowable in certain circumstances but never in others. We will consider specific examples later.

Definition of trademark use (who owns a given trademark)

An article sold and shipped across at least one state line with the trademark actually attached to it meets the PTO's definition of putting the trademark into use in interstate commerce. In the eyes of the law, what establishes your right to employ a given trademark is your being the *first to use the mark in commerce* (in interstate commerce, in the case of the federal government; in intrastate commerce, in the case of the state). Registration of the mark provides many advantages, as we shall see, but it is not legally required. An unregistered mark can still be successfully defended against infringement, although with much greater difficulty than a registered one. Unless the trademark appears *on* the goods themselves, it does not meet the criteria. With regard to manufactured goods, the mark must appear physically in some manner on the goods themselves, either placed directly on the goods, on displays associated with the goods, or on tags or labels attached to the goods. With regard to services, the "attachment" is less concrete, of course, but the mark must be connected with the service through advertising or some other form of association, as in brochures about the services or on business cards or stationery used in connection with the services.

24

Registration process

If you decide to register your trademark or service mark that is already in use, you will need to file an application with the PTO (See Appendix C for this form). The current cost of such an application is $175 for each class of goods or services for which the application is made. (The intent-to-use application, discussed on page 23, also requires a $175 fee.) Your application will then be examined by the staff to see if it conforms to the requirements of the Trademark Act, the most basic of which is that the mark not so resemble another mark in use as to cause confusion, mistake, or deception when used on similar or related goods. Trademark examination currently takes about 3 months to complete. The applicant must respond to any objections raised by the examiners within 6 months. If the use-based mark is deemed to be registrable, it will be published for opposition, as already noted, in the trademark section of the *Official Gazette*. If no one files a challenge to it within 30 days, or a challenge is made but proves unsuccessful, the trademark is considered valid and is registered for 10 years. (The previous 20-year registration period has been halved to eliminate any "dead wood" more quickly—trademarks registered and never used or used only briefly.) An affidavit of continued use in commerce will have to be filed between the fifth and sixth years following the registration date to keep the registration. As long as the mark continues in use, the registration can be renewed every 10 years, without limit.

Once the intent-to-use application is filed and a Notice of Allowance issued (see page 23), a second step is required for registration. The applicant must actually make use of the mark in commerce *before* a registration will be issued. After use begins, the applicant must submit, along with specimens showing use and a fee of $100 per class of goods or services in the application, either (1) an Amendment to Allege Use or (2) a Statement of Use. The difference between these two filings is the timing of the filing. See Appendix C for a copy of these forms and an explanation of when to use each one.

Waiting period

There is no minimum or maximum waiting period from the time of first putting the trademark or service mark into use until filing an application to register it with the PTO (in the case of the use-based application). In the event of a dispute, the first one to use the trademark is considered the rightful owner, even if he or she was not the first to apply for registration. Since

priority of use is the sole test of ownership, the first user of a mark, even if it is not well known to the public, will prevail in the case of legal conflict.

Registration optional; use of ™ and ®

It is not necessary to register a trademark at all in order to protect your rights in it. You may use the symbol ™ (trademark) or SM (service mark) after the name in question, regardless of whether or not you have registered the mark on the state and/or federal level. By contrast, it is illegal to use the symbol ® unless a registration on the federal level has actually been carried out. Such a falsification may bar the mark's subsequent registration, with the loss of any protection against infringers. Other ways of indicating that the mark *is* registered include use of the phrases "Registered in U.S. Patent and Trademark Office" or "Reg. U.S. Pat. & Tm. Off."

There are definite advantages to registration on the Principal Register,[1] which we will now take a look at.

---

[1] There also exists a Supplemental Register for marks that do not meet the criteria for registration on the Principal Register; the Supplemental Register offers more limited advantages, which we will consider below.

Advantages of registration on the Principal Register

A federal trademark registration offers a number of advantages over and above those provided by common law rights and by a state registration. Chief among these are:

1. Registration, followed by publication in the *Official Gazette*, provides constructive notice to the public of your ownership of and exclusive right to use the mark. Your registration eliminates a good faith defense for a party adopting the trademark subsequent to your date of registration.

2. Registration gives you the right to sue an infringer in federal court, without the need to meet a required disputed amount and with a minimum of delay. No proof—and the lengthy legal proceedings needed to establish it—of the right to exclusive use of the name is needed. The trademark registrant only has to enter his or her certificate of registration as evidence of the rightful ownership of the name. Other legal rights accorded by federal jurisdiction include: the right to obtain an injunction, enforceable by any U.S. district court, against an infringer; the right to recover lost profits plus damages, including treble damages for attorney fees; the right to have infringing labels destroyed.

3. Your registration will become incontestible, provided it is not successfully challenged within five years from the filing date of your application. Given the uncertainties surrounding much trademark usage, the value of such incontestability is not to be underestimated.

4. Your registration can be filed with the U.S. Customs Service to prevent goods with infringing marks from entering the country. Each year, millions of dollars of such goods with illegal marks, many of them mimicking famous trademarks, are seized and destroyed by the Customs Service. Without registration, the legal proceedings necessary to effect the barring of entry of goods with infringing or counterfeit marks would be particularly burdensome.

5. Registration gives you the additional protection of the availability of criminal penalties against an infringer in an action for counterfeiting a registered trademark.

6. Your U.S. registration provides a basis for filing trademark applications in foreign countries under the Paris Convention.

Many businesses that market their products or services nationally not only register their marks with the PTO, but also with the state(s) in which they do business. Trademark registrations in California and New York have proven themselves especially valuable. While state registration offers protection against infringers only in the jurisdiction of that individual state, these two large, important states have taken a particularly strong, protective stance in favor of the trademark registrant who does business in their jurisdiction. Antidilution legislation in California and New York forbids adoption of a commercial name which is the same as or similar to one already in use, even in areas completely unrelated to the original usage. Since this type of law in essence prevents the same word from serving as a trademark for two or more different, unrelated kinds of goods, it proves in fact to be much more stringent than even the federal legislative protections.

Trade names not registrable

It is very important to note that trade names per se *cannot* be registered with the PTO, although such names enjoy the same legal protection as trademarks and service marks. Furthermore, many trade names serve a dual purpose. The same name not only designates a company, but it also serves to distinguish a product or product line or a service. MARS, INC. and INTERNATIONAL BUSINESS MACHINES, INC. cannot be registered. MARS, as in MARS bar, and IBM as a trademark appearing on computers *are* registrable marks, however. The tipoff is any name which has a word like "Incorporated," "Limited," "Company," or a similar term or abbreviation as a part of it. Such names will usually fail the registration test. The same name, without the Inc. or Co., when used to designate a product or service, will be registrable, provided it meets certain other tests as well. In order to use your corporate name as a trademark (or service mark), you should also avoid listing your business address together with the name on the goods in question and avoid using the name with such phrases as "made by " or "manufactured by." It is advisable, whenever possible, to follow the trademark with the generic name of the product, such as APPLE computer. A portion of the corporate name may often be used effectively as a trademark if it is combined with a design element. GAUSS ELECTROPHYSICS, INC., for example, created a registrable trademark distinct from its commercial

name by combining the name "GAUSS" with a logo.

To obtain the same advantages provided by federal registration for your *trade name*, which is not in itself registrable, plan to use part of the trade name as a trade mark or service mark. Almost all large companies, from GENERAL MOTORS to IBM—and many astute smaller companies as well—use this tactic to legally protect two forms of commercial name (a trade name and a mark) with one linguistic shield.

E ven if the *only* business name you will ever need is your trade name, and it will not serve a dual role as a trademark or service mark, you are not free to choose any name you wish. If your trade name conflicts with someone else's trade name, trademark or service mark, you may still be held legally liable. Therefore, even though your trade name is not registrable by the PTO, you must exercise the same care in selecting it as you would a trademark or service mark, for trade names are legally protected in the same way as trademarks and service marks.

If yours is a small company with one product, there is often a tremendous tactical advantage in having the company name the same as the product name. Each time one is mentioned in print, the other one will automatically be invoked as well, giving you needed additional exposure.

Genericide

T here exists the curious case of trademarks or service marks that were once registrable but that have lost their right to registration because of too great popularity. These are commercial names that, because the particular brands proved so successful, ended up being completely identifed in the public perception with *all* products of that class. Aspirin, cellophane, milk of magnesia, celluloid, linoleum, shredded wheat, lanolin, kerosene, thermos,[2] and mimeograph all met this fate, which has been termed "genericide," and their respective manufacturers lost the right to exclusive use of the name to designate their product. The name became public property, a generic term available to anyone and everyone. While small businesses do not normally have this problem, it is one that major companies with hugely successful products, such as Xerox, Frigidaire, Coke, and Kleenex, have to contend with.

Certification marks and collective marks

In addition to trademarks and service marks, there are two other classes of marks recognized by the PTO. These are certification marks, which provide "seals of approval" for products (such as that offered by GOOD HOUSEKEEPING), and collective marks, used by members of associations (on stationery, for example) to denote their membership in a particular group. Having acknowledged the existence of these two specialized types of marks, they need not concern us further at this time. All four types of marks—trademarks, service marks, certification marks, and collective marks—are legally protected from infringement. All four appear in the computer data base named TRADEMARKSCAN, which we will consider later in regard to doing trademark searches.

---

2   Curiously, trademark rights may be lost in this fashion in one country but not in another. Such is the case with "thermos" and "cellophane," both of which remain valid (and valued) trademarks in Great Britain, although the words long ago became genericized in the United States.

Seven types of commercial marks

The bewildering array of marks used in commerce can be broken down into a few basic categories. As we shall see, certain types of words, when used as trademarks or service marks or trade names, have distinct advantages over other types. We will briefly survey the use of names, whether personal or geographic, common English words, foreign words, puns, coined words, and numbers, initials, and acronyms as commercial marks. While these categories do not include all possible types of trade names, trade marks, and service marks, they cover a great number of the commercial names in use.

Personal names

In the past, the most common type of trademark or trade name in use was a man's own name (CANNON, SQUIBB, KELLOGG, GERBER, WOOLWORTH). Today, this is one of the least desirable forms of commercial name, for reasons that will be discussed below. A mark may also be the name of a famous person (other than yourself!), who is either living or dead (ESTÉE LAUDER, GLORIA VANDERBILT, HALSTON, LINCOLN). It may be a literary or mythological allusion to a person (PETER PAN, AJAX, JUPITER), a biblical reference or a saint's name (SAMSON, ST. MARTIN), or a fictitious person or 'critter' created solely for the purpose of promoting a particular product or line (AUNT JEMIMA, MR. PEANUT, ANN PAGE, CHARLIE THE TUNA, THE GREEN GIANT).

Geographic names

In certain circumstances, a commercial name may consist of a geographic name which truly indicates the source of origin of a product (WATERFORD crystal, ELGIN watches). Many geographic names do not really denote origin, however, but are used in an arbitrary or whimsical fashion, as in the case of MALIBU and SALEM cigarettes or DUTCH BOY paint. More will be said about this important distinction later.

Everyday English words

Trade names or marks may also be common words adopted to contexts either related to or ironically unrelated to their original meaning (DIEHARD batteries, BICYCLE playing cards, ARROW shirts, TOMATO bank). This type of commercial name offers some of the greatest possibilities for creativity and humor.

Foreign words

Foreign words, whose meaning is often expressive of the product's design or function, supply other marks (CORONA, CARIOCA, LUCITE, DRAMAMINE). Latin and Greek words and their derivates make up a subcategory of foreign words used in commerce that is particularly suited for a specialty market or audience consisting of the highly educated. Made-up words that *look* foreign and that also have favorable foreign connotations are a relatively recent discovery that present another option for commercial naming: ATARI, PRIAZZO.

Puns

While a name that uses a pun for its effect may fall into one of the other categories as well, its play on words also sets it apart, producing a humorous effect. In general, a pun creates a humorous juxtaposition between the name and some familiar figure of speech, as in PLUM LOCO (the name of a brand of preserves). TEX'S CHAIN SAW MANICURE, an unforgettable name for a tree- and yard-care service, is a prize winner in this category. [3]

Coined words

Some coined words are suggestive, implying something about the nature of the product or company (COMPAQ, KLEENEX, NYQUIL, NABISCO). Other coined words, having absolutely no meaning (EXXON, XEROX), offer other possibilities of choice.

Numbers, initials, and acronyms

There are trademarks consisting only of numbers (4711 [a cologne], 1-2-3 [computer software], TI 99/4 [a computer], 240 [a car made by MERCEDES-BENZ], 273 [a perfume]). There exist many trademarks composed only of initials (GE, RCA, NBC), which, in many cases, consist of the first letters of the words making up a longer name. NBC, for example, is simply an abbreviated form of NATIONAL BROADCASTING CORPORATION. Other names in this category represent a combination of numbers and initials (A-1 sauce, for example).

---

3   **A new book by Dennis Baron, *Declining Grammar* (Urbana, Illinois: National Council of Teachers of English, 1990) lists over 100 business names that are based on clever (or not so clever) puns, including The Brick Shirt House, Let's Pet (a petstore), and Ladies First (a gynecological practice).**

Criteria for an acceptable mark

In general, your proposed trademark or service mark cannot be confusingly similar to any other mark previously registered or used by someone else. Of course, what this allows or disallows hinges upon the interpretation of the term "confusingly similar." A confusingly similar mark is regarded by the PTO as one which would be *likely* to make buyers suppose that there is some connection between the two products or manufacturers when, in fact, none exists.

It is your duty to survey the field of possibilities of already existing trademarks, service marks, and trade names to the best of your ability and to choose a mark which will avoid confusion with others already in use. The practical aspects of this selection process will involve weighing both the relationship between the types of goods or services involved as well as the attributes of the mark itself.

Some trademarks, termed "strong" marks, are so powerful that the use of the same name or a similar one to designate *any other product* is disallowed. KODAK is the classic example of such a strong mark, which cannot be used to name any other goods or products, not just camera equipment and supplies. An individual who attempted to trademark "Kodak" as a brand name for cigarette lighters was rebuffed by the PTO, under the assumption that any other user of the name infringes on the rights of the Eastman Kodak Company. By contrast, other marks, termed "weak" marks, appear in identical or near-identical form on thousands of similar goods. Terms such as "Ace," "Imperial," "Elite," and "Supreme" fall into this category. In this case, the range of the trademark is exceedingly narrow. The exact name cannot normally be used to designate identical goods but may be applied to many areas of similar goods. More will be said about the characteristics of strong v. weak marks in the section on selecting a name below.

Use of obscene and scandalous marks forbidden

Certain types of marks are automatically excluded from use by the PTO and must be avoided. Into this category fall obscene and scandalous marks. (If in doubt about whether a mark is obscene or scandalous, ask your mother!) Although this discussion is not concerned with design, it is significant to note that designs that simulate the flag of any country or the emblems of certain organizations are also not allowed.

Use of your family name disallowed (well, almost always)

I t is the general policy of the PTO to disallow any one person from trademarking a family name and thus preventing all others with the same last name from using their own surnames in a competing business. One obvious exception to this general rule does, in fact, exist. If it so happens that a family name has *already* been employed to such a degree that it has become linked, in the public perception, with *one* source for a particular product, it can then be registered. Five years' substantially exclusive and continuous usage is generally regarded as proof of this connection between the family name and a particular brand or service. What this means is that *no one* in that period of time can open a business designated by the same name in the particular area of business you have chosen, say, household furniture, or you will lose the right to its exclusive use. If yours is a common surname, the likelihood of no one else starting a business with the same name in the same field anywhere in the United States in a five-year period may be remote indeed. You will still be entitled to use your name in connection with your company, of course. You will simply not have exclusive use. The other Smith who has opened a competing store under his name (your estranged cousin!) will forever after be diluting the value of your business name with his identically named stores. If his store has rats coming out of the woodwork and shoddy merchandise, his bad reputation may very well tarnish yours as well.

Although most trademarks in the past consisted of family surnames (SINGER, THE SMITH BROTHERS, GILLETTE), today, given the explosion of products and services in the marketplace, it is virtually impossible to name your business after yourself and hope to gain exclusive use to the name by means of a trademark.

If your name is highly unusual, Mr. Ziefoursoundrylicki, there are equally strong business reasons to avoid naming the company with your patronym. What happens if you decide to sell your business? The buyer may not want the company to carry your name. You, on the other hand, may have strong misgivings about selling the value of your good name to a new owner, who may prove unscrupulous. If the buyer does choose to keep your name, with your permission, will you be able to open another business under your own name? In all likelihood, no. What about your relatives with the same surname? If the name of the business has to be changed at the time of sale, there will, in all likelihood, be unfavorable tax consequences.

The case of TAYLOR wines is instructive. The family sold the TAYLOR WINE CO. to the COCA-COLA CO. but continued to use their family name to promote their own line of wines. After a legal suit by COCA-COLA, however, a federal appeals court barred the Taylor family from ever again using the Taylor name in connection with wine.

One of the cases today when the advantages of a family name to designate a business would outweigh any egoistic disadvantages would be if the name is of such a character as to transcend its origins. Names that lend themselves well to graphic rendering or that have positive connotations may be particularly well suited for trademarks. The example of BIRDSEYE, a brand of frozen vegetables, is a case in point. Few not knowledgeable about the source of the name would guess that the brand is named after Clarence Birdseye, who developed a technique of preserving fresh vegetables by freezing them. This particular name lends itself well to a trademark function, with its familiar pictorial depiction of a stylized bird forming the black backdrop of the lettering of the name itself. The family name of CANNON likewise provided an excellent trademark, with pictorial representation, in spite of the unlikely juxtaposition of towels with the name and drawing of a military weapon. Other surnames, such as GOODYEAR

(the name of the inventor of a product, who was *not* the founder of the company), also function as effective trade names and trademarks because the names suggest certain positive values over and above their designation of particular families. If your last name is Birdwhistle and you are planning on opening a pet shop that sells exotic birds, the positive connotations of your surname as the business name in such a case may very well outweigh other negative considerations.

Use of names other than your own

Trademarks which are the names of famous actual persons can in fact be registered, with the written consent of the person in question. The Patent and Trademark Office has a specific form to be filled out by the applicant seeking a trademark of this sort. These types of trademarks normally involve the payment of royalties by the companies using the marks to the individuals involved, if they are still living (or to their estates if they are recently deceased), as in the case of MAX FACTOR, ESTÉE LAUDER, GLORIA VANDERBILT, SASSON, HALSTON, and DIANE VON FURSTENBERG, all trademarks based on the names of famous real life persons. The GLORIA VANDERBILT trademark recently changed hands for $15 million.

Geographic names

A geographic name which is descriptive of the origin of goods or services cannot be registered as a trademark, generally speaking, unless it can be shown to have become distinctive in the same way that family surnames can, through exclusive use, as in the example of the Fords or the Gillettes. WATERFORD crystal and ELGIN watches have met the test of time, but others will succeed in doing so only with difficulty. You will have to prove a minimum of at least five years' *exclusive* use of the name before being granted registration by the PTO. The rationale behind this policy is the same as that for surnames. No business has the right to take a geographically descriptive term out of the public domain for its exclusive use if others also wish to use it in a commercial context as well. If such a procedure were permitted without reservation, then one potato grower could, for example, adopt the term "Idaho" for his sole use. If no one else could inform the public that his tulips were Dutch, that his rum was Jamaican, and so on, except for the original registrant of the descriptive geographic name, then communication about the source of products would be severely impeded indeed.

Geographically descriptive terms can range from the name of a single building (MAXWELL HOUSE, a hotel) to that of an entire continent (NORTH AMERICAN VAN LINES), and everything in between: that of a nation (More than five hundred businesses have the word "American" as the first word in their name), a region (MIDWEST CHEESE COMPANY), a state (ILLINOIS TOOL WORKS, INC.), a city (CHICAGO CAT CLINIC) or an area of a city (MID-CITY ICE CREAM CO.).

Many geographic allusions used in commercial names imply *nothing* about the origin of the product or service, however. These are not subject to the same legal trademark requirements as geographic names that are truly descriptive of the source of goods or services. The owners of such names do not have to prove five

38

years of continuous use in order to register them as trademarks. AVON products, for example, named after a river in England, employs a geographic allusion but not in a descriptive fashion (the name is used whimsically, since it implies nothing about the source of the products as somehow connected with the Avon River). MALIBU cigarettes and DUTCH BOY paints likewise contain geographic allusions that are used in a nondescriptive, arbitrary fashion, since they tell us nothing about the source of the products in question. MALIBU cigarettes are actually manufactured by an American tobacco company and DUTCH BOY paints, as we are well aware, do not originate in Holland.

A geographic term which is used in a deceptive sense to imply a false origin is not registrable or protectable as a trademark. A watch made in Wisconsin could not bear the trademark of SWISS watch, for example.

Descriptiveness exclusion

Trademarks which merely describe products are not registrable, unless they attain distinctiveness through long-term exclusive use, like family names and geographic terms discussed above. A popular Chicago weekly newspaper named *The Reader* did not pass muster, since its name was considered simply descriptive of what all newspapers normally invite their readers to do. In the case of the Convenience Store chain, registration of the name was also denied on similar grounds. The court ruled that the word "convenient" was generic, in effect denying the company exclusive rights to the name. One Convenience subfranchiser legally challenged his obligation to pay franchise fees at all, his contention being that the fees are in essence charged for the use of the name. Since the name has proven unregistrable as a trademark, he and his subfranchisees have dropped the Convenient name from their stores altogether and are using a new one—"BONFARE." Because of the problems arising from its business name and the resulting loss of revenues, the Convenience Store chain ended up filing for bankruptcy. It goes to show how a poor name choice, in the right circumstances, can lead to disaster. If a mark is merely suggestive of the product instead of descriptive (LUSTRE for shampoo, for example), it *is* acceptable and registrable as a trademark.

Satiric, ironic, and parodic names

Trademarks chosen to parody or satirize a well-known existing brand of goods or services crop up very often. LARDASHE jeans for overweight people derives its appeal as a name from its being a clever take-off on JORDACHE jeans. DOGIVA dog biscuits was a playful rearrangement of the GODIVA brand of chocolates. And MIAMI MICE T-shirts sporting macho mice cartoon characters is an obvious spoof of a popular TV series. The only problem with such trademarks as these is that they have a low success rate for standing up in court. For the parody to be effective, it must be aimed at a famous product. But companies that put out such popular merchandise are precisely the ones with the most legal clout. Don't imagine that the company you are spoofing will share your sense of humor. *Au contraire*, they will, in most cases, haul you off to court and do everything in their power to prevent your use of what they consider a perversion of *their* property. In instances such as these, the main legal argument rests upon "dilution," the claim that your similar use of the name "dilutes" the effectiveness of their trademark or service mark.

So be forewarned. If you have come up with the century's most hilarious take-off on someone else's name, go ahead if you must. But you will almost certainly have to face a legal battle—perhaps a series of them—over the choice of name, and your chances of winning are uncertain. LARDASHE jeans, by the way, did stand up in court; DOGIVA and MIAMI MICE did not.

Principal and Supplemental Registers

It was previously mentioned that two federal registers for trademarks exist, the Principal Register and the Supplemental Register. Normally, anyone attempting to register a trademark on the federal level aims for the Principal Register, since it provides a wide range of protections against infringers. In general, marks that are coined words, whether nonsensical (such as KODAK) or suggestive (such as NYQUIL), and ones that are common English words, whether fanciful (such as BICYCLE for playing cards), or suggestive (SURE for deodorant), qualify for registration on the Principal Register (provided they are not confusingly similar to a previously registered mark). Names which do not meet the requirements for registration on this register, such as surnames, geographic names that denote the source of origin, and names which are merely descriptive, can still be recorded on the Supplemental Register. Such marks, while they do not meet all the tests of a trademark, are distinctive enough to be capable of distinguishing the origins of one's goods or services.

The Supplemental Register permits a broad range of marks, phrases, slogans, labels, symbols, containers, and configurations of goods to be recorded for public record. Also, marks on the Supplemental Register may, in time, acquire a distinctiveness which qualifies them as true trademarks and allows them to be registered on the Principal Register.

The chief advantages of registration on the Supplemental Register are these:

(1) The registrant may bring suit for trademark infringement in the federal courts.
(2) If your business will be involved in foreign commerce, the basis for foreign trademark registration will usually be prior registration in your own country. Under the Paris Convention, the Supplemental Register fulfills this requirement.
(3) In the event your business is sold, registration on the Supplemental Register will provide the legal basis for the transfer of goodwill and trademark(s) of the business.

We saw

that there is no waiting period before applying for registration of a mark on the Principal Register. A complete year's use of the mark in commerce *is* required prior to filing an application for registration on the Supplemental Register, however. If you first file an application for the Principal Register, and it is thereafter transferred to the Supplemental Register, no additional filing fee is necessary, and the full year's usage may be dated back to the date of transfer.

Part 2: The Mechanics And Aesthetics Of Business Names

The name selection process: summary and overview

We have already noted the types of commercial names that are usually best avoided: names that are merely descriptive or generic, family surnames, geographic names that denote actual source or origin, and names identical to or deceptively similar to ones already in use to designate the same or similar classes of goods. To this list should also be added "initials" as a type of name best left to the large conglomerates. Although initials are generally a poor choice for a smaller company name for a number of reasons, they are used with surprising frequency and with predictable results, producing a name that is neither distinctive nor memorable. Not only do initials lack individuality, they are also difficult to find in the telephone directory, and they are rarely acceptable as registrable trademarks. Some notable exceptions will immediately come to mind. But you must remember that the RCAs and the IBMs of the world have millions to spend on promotional advertising and thus can *create* distinctiveness for their commercial monikers. If you name your business DUD Enterprises, will you have a similar budget to promote your name to the public?

We have also already pointed out some of the major types of commercial names that are commercially effective and legally defendable: names using common English words (BICYCLE, GREYHOUND, BANTAM), coined names that are suggestive (NYQUIL), coined names that are meaningless (KODAK, EXXON), fanciful geographic names (MALIBU), and personal names other than your own (NAPOLEON, LINCOLN).

45

Six Approaches to Naming

Now that you have a basic idea of what works and what to avoid in the area of commercial naming, how do you, the business owner, come up with an effective name to designate your company, your products, or your services? Experience shows that there is no one route to a successful name. An intuition may sometimes produce a solution that compares favorably with the most rigorous market research. Let us consider some approaches that have yielded results.

Contests

One popular tactic is the name-that-_____ contest, which may be open to the public or simply involve employees of the business. This type of competitive exercise is best suited to already operating businesses that want to produce a new name. The contest, if handled properly, can become a highly successful promotional event which focuses dramatic attention on a particular business's profile in the marketplace. At least a modest prize will have to be offered for the best name presented, but this expenditure will repay its cost many times over in terms of goodwill and increased awareness, by employees and the general public, of the activities of the company. There is no assurance, of course, that this approach will yield a usable name, but, in many cases, this consideration is not really as important as it might seem. The contest focuses attention on the *search* for a new name. Its primary value is in setting the wheels in motion, regardless of whether in itself it produces the final end result. Although the best name suggested will have to be awarded a prize, the name itself may well be judged later on to be inappropriate or prove legally unsound.

One famous case of an award-winning name selected through this avenue was that of BABY RUTH, submitted by an employee of the CURTIS CANDY CO. in a naming contest. The name proved immensely popular and helped to make the candy the best-selling brand of nut bar in the country. The candy was not, incidentally, named after the homerun king, but rather the first daughter of President and Mrs. Grover Cleveland, who was affectionately known as "Baby Ruth."

The SAFEWAY Supermarket chain also selected its name from a public competition. The CHEMSTRAND CORPORATION relied upon a contest to name its synthetic fiber, ACRILAN. A contest resulted in the MR. PEANUT logo as well. The original drawing was submitted by a school boy, and was developed into the animated peanut wearing top hat and cane and monicle, which became the hugely successful logo of PLANTERS PEANUTS.

Computer-generated words

Today, a popular approach to commercial naming is the use of a computer program to generate lists of potential names, according to certain guidelines. While computers can play a role in name creation, it is important to remember that the work that the computer does is purely mechanical. It can give you lists of hundreds or thousands of words meeting certain specifications (say, words of two syllables or less, each starting with an E or D or T, and containing an X), but the human imagination is indispensable in sorting the wheat from the chaff. The SALINON CORP. of Dallas sells NAMER, a reasonably priced computer program designed to assist in business name selection. The use of such a program can help to get the creative juices flowing, although it cannot by itself yield the final solution. Some well-known name factories, such as San Francisco-based NAMELAB, use computers with their own customized software to come up with a long list of possible name choices, which are then narrowed to a few by individual employees of the company.

Shotgun approach

This approach follows the procedure of collecting potential names from all possible sources—dreams, the neighbor's children, free association, friends' suggestions. A long list may be compiled, and then a narrowing to a few deemed most appropriate is tried. Such impressionistic attempts usually fail because the collector(s) has(have) no clear guidelines of choice. By casting one's nets too widely, one snares many minnows but no prize-winning fish. This approach works best if allied with some rigorous spade work in which one clearly defines one's market and the most significant attributes of one's product or service. An appeal to the irrational, the unconscious, the whimsical will yield its most dramatic results for the prepared mind that knows all the intricacies of the business or product or service that requires a name.

The use of ad hoc consultants... Those who are fascinated by the power of words can often be relied upon to supply helpful input, whether formally (for money) or informally (gratis). Word mavens, including Scrabble zealots, word puzzle buffs, and professional writers, are among those whom you might approach for advice.

Committee approach

The committee selection process is frequently tried as a level-headed, no-nonsense approach to commercial naming. A group of individuals involved with the company, either as incorporators in the case of a start-up business or officer-directors in the instance of a going concern, put their heads together to try to come up with a suitable name. There is a great deal to be said for synergy, the power produced by the meeting of minds. It is important to have clearly in hand the criteria that such a search must adhere to, however. If none of the minds in question is oriented in what to look for, none of the names produced by such brainstorming sessions may be workable. The danger of such an approach is that individuals who, as a group, have some stake in the selection process, may let this vested interest blind them to the fact that they may have *absolutely* no knowledge of what steps to follow in order to come up with an effective name. This approach most often proves unsatisfactory for the same reason as the shotgun approach. It may generate many possibilities but does not know how to appraise them as to relative worth.

Creation of a song or advertisement

In many cases, trademarks have developed out of an advertisement or song written to promote a particular product. For this reason, Henri Charmasson, a well-known associate of ALIAS, a name consulting firm in San Diego, strongly advocates the writing of a commercial in which the proposed name of a product or service will be featured.[1] Experience has shown that the dramatization of the product or service in a commercial setting often does crystallize the name that is being sought. Consider the case of CHIQUITA bananas. This trademark developed from a song written to promote the bananas of the UNITED FRUIT COMPANY. The song featured a singing banana, much like the California Raisins of contemporary fame. ("I'm Chiquita banana and I've come to say/Bananas have to ripen in a certain way . . ."). This particular trademark proved so successful that the UNITED FRUIT COMPANY placed the CHIQUITA mark on all its produce. In this way, a dull, descriptive trade name was supplanted by an imaginative one with personality and pizazz. This same process of name selection can be tapped by anyone. Try writing a song or advertisement about your product or service. Even though you have no intention of ever using it, you may very well arrive, through this act of creative thinking, at the perfect name.

A voice crying in the wilderness

The linguistically savvy individual, equipped with a few basic principles, often proves to be the most effective name-finder or creator of all. If you are a literate person who can read and write and who is attuned to the nuances of words, you can do an effective name selection. You are already miles ahead, in fact, of many of those entrusted with such matters, from the smallest proprietorship or partnership to some of the largest corporate conglomerates.

The force of one mind finely focused on the particular task at hand is often far greater than all the high-powered panels of professionals that money can buy.

With a few basic guidelines, you should be able to do what most companies have not succeeded in doing, namely create a commercial identifier for your business or its goods or services that is distinctive and memorable. Through the choice of an outstanding name, you can immediately position your business for dominance in a given market. Your selection of a name will immediately set the tone for your business undertaking, predestining it, in many cases, for success—or failure.

---

1   See Henri Charmasson, *The Name Is the Game: How to Name a Company or Product* (Homewood, Illinois: Dow Jones-Irwin, 1988), Chapter 8.

Regardless of whether

the name selection process is being carried out by a group or one individual principally, the following suggestions should be taken into consideration.

First, do not expect the ideal name to come to you in a blinding flash of insight. Before the United States trademark field (not to mention the international one) was cluttered with some million registered marks and many more unregistered ones, the business owner could wait for that serendipitous moment of inspiration. Nowadays, the successful name hunter must adopt a more analytical and structured approach to successfully trap his linguistic quarry. The final selection may very well result from a moment of "Eureka!" But such insights always tend to favor the prepared, not the unprepared, mind and the carefully thought out, not the haphazard, approach.

In arriving at an acceptable trade name, trademark or service mark, you may either plan to come up with a list of possible names, ranked in order of preference, or simply one that best fits the job that you require of it. In either case, you will then need to turn your attention to the legal criteria which we will examine in detail in Part 3. If the name you desire proves to be already in use, you will then go to the next preference on your list or come up with another name if you are working with your one best shot.

The following discussion will flesh out the means at your disposal in selecting an appropriate name, one in which sense and sound are ideally wedded.

The Medium: Potential Sources of New Names

1. The "as is" English word

The English language provides a vast pool of names for commercial purposes, a seemingly unending supply of words which can be adopted without change to designate a product or service or organization. The only drawback to this source for business names is that, like the favorite fishing hole, it has been used so often and so steadily that it no longer supplies the impressive "catches" it once did. The need for a continual stream of new commercial identifiers in our highly commercially developed society has taken more and more words out of circulation. The resources of the language are quickly being exhausted in this way. Today, a careful search must be conducted to determine if the proposed word is available for the purpose intended.

One advantage of this approach to naming—pressing a common English word into service—is that the same word can be (and generally is) used for many different categories of goods or services provided by different, unrelated companies. Take the word "Cascade," for instance. Virtually everyone knows that it is the brand name for a type of detergent in use in automatic dishwashers. But the exact same word designates many other products as well. To cite but one example, CASCADE is also a brand name for a type of photocopy paper produced by another company, the BOISE CASCADE COMPANY (and here we see the same word appearing as part of the company trade name as well). Again, everyone is familiar

50

with ARROW shirts, but do you know how many other products manufactured by other companies are named "Arrow"? Literally dozens. The *one* item that cannot effectively be designated by this word in the business world is, of course, that thing with a sharp tip and a long shaft normally shot with a bow at a target, yet this kind of redundancy is what many businesses actually engage in when called upon to find a suitable business name.

Besides the warning that a name chosen from the English language, without modification, to do duty as a commercial moniker must be searched according to the procedures outlined in Part 3 below, an additional caution is in order. Some names of this type have built up such a distinctiveness that the courts have ruled that no other company can use the same word in a commerical context. This is the exception that proves the rule, since most words can safely be used by many different industries to designate different goods or services. It is important to know that it can also happen that one company, through long and continued use, can develop a virtual monopoly on an English word, used as a trade name or trademark, or both, as in the case of GREYHOUND. The word came to be so closely associated with the bus company that a financial services firm that wished to use the same name was legally barred from doing so.

A good rule of thumb is that if the Patent and Trademark Office has already registered the same word to designate several different brands of goods or services, the word can generally be adopted to designate still other goods and services as well, provided they are not *related.**

*Related goods: Goods are deemed to be related if they are used together, they are sold together, they are sold to a similar class or group of purchasers, or they are marketed through the same channels of trade, whether through direct marketing, the consumer retail trade, the industrial-institutional network, and so on. Any or all of these factors would contribute to a buyer's (mistaken) perception that two products having the same or a similar mark derive from a common source. The more closely related the goods in question, the more distinctive the marks must be.

2. The altered English word

A number of techniques exist for changing a basic English word in order to create a new word to be used in commerce. The most common of these techniques involves:

(1) adding a prefix or suffix to an already existing word
(2) joining two or more words together by overlapping a common element, or
(3) "gluing" two or more words together to create a new term.

The procedure of adding something to an already existing word involves the use of prefixes or suffixes such as -ette, porta-, -matic, pro-, -flex, -pro, tele-, uni-, meta-, and iso- .
Examples: STYLETTE, PORTA-GRILL, MAXI MOUSE, TELECROS

The joining of two or more words together by overlapping common elements is a less common but equally effective technique of name generation.
Examples: STYLEDGE, STRIPPLEASE

The "gluing" of two or more words together to create a new term often, although not always, results in a hyphenated name.
Examples: PALMOLIVE, MILK-BONE, HONEY-COMB, KIMBERLEY-CLARK

"A commercial name that is any good is scary"—Ira Bachrach, founder of NameLab, a San Francisco-based name factory.

3. Coined words

Another type of commercial name involves the creation of a new word which may be either suggestive or completely meaningless. NYQUIL is a classic example of the first case, KODAK of the second. The coined term NYQUIL suggests the nature of the product it designates, namely a medicine designed to induce night-time tranquility, while KODAK carries no apparent meaning at all.

4. Abandoned names

Another somewhat unusual source for commercial names involves neither the adoption of a common English word to an uncommon context nor the modification of an English word, the combination of two or more words, or the coining of a new word. You can legally take as your own a name which has been abandoned by someone else. A large percentage of commerical names does fall into disuse for one reason or another, making them fair game for someone else. TRADEMARKSCAN indicates the marks which have been abandoned and subsequently cancelled by the PTO, going back to 1984. When a company abandons a particular trade name or product name, furthermore, it is even possible for another company to take up the discarded name and use it as its own. Larger companies will normally make a formal public announcement of a particular trade name or mark's abandonment, leaving it up for grabs. Whether such a tactic is advisable or not must be determined under particular circumstances, but abandoned names, particularly those previously owned by large corporations, do offer one more source for potentially lucrative commercial identifiers as well as product or service marks.

53

5. Foreign words

Another relatively untapped source of names for use in commerce is the foreign word or phrase, whose meaning would ordinarily be suggestive of the product or service or appealing to the audience for which it is intended. Such a choice of name might well be appropriate for niche marketing to a particular ethnic group. Consider the example of BON AMI, the name for such a mundane item as a cleanser, sold to a clearly defined ethnic market. John T. Robertson termed his cleanser Robertson's Mineral Soap. Later, the stockholders of the rapidly expanding company, whose scouring powder was sold primarily to French-Canadian housewives, renamed it BON AMI ("Good Friend"), to good effect.

Latin and Greek words and their derivations comprise a special category of commercial naming. Words from these classical languages, generally speaking, are usually most appropriate in designating products marketed to the highly educated—physicians, scientists, academics. Many prescription drugs not marketed directly to the public carry names derived from Latin or Greek (NEODECADRON and PROTROPIN, for example). By contrast, an over-the-counter medication would not be likely to do well with such a name. To be sure, some products intended for the general public, such as DRAMAMINE and LUCITE, do sport Latin- or Greek-based nomenclature. But these represent the exception instead of the rule. French and Italian words used as brand names generally connote sophistication to an English-speaking audience. A French word might be particularly appropriate as a name for a perfume or an article of clothing, for example. We have already noted another recent development, the fake foreign name, such as ATARI, which sounds Japanese but, in fact, is a made-up word.

6. "Stolen" names

Sometimes, effective names have been taken from other products and recycled. This borrowing tactic only works with 'weak' marks, needless to say. The name for CARNATION evaporated milk, for example, was suggested by CARNATION brand cigars. When you consider that the word IVORY not only designates a brand of soap but some 200 other brands of goods, it would appear that a great deal of "borrowing" is going on. If you find a word already in use that fits to a T the item you need to name, don't automatically assume that this name is already taken and thus off limits. In many instances, the same name can be 'borrowed' and reused by someone else to designate a different, unrelated line of merchandise or service.

To cite but one more case, DOMINO'S pizza carries the same name as another well-known Domino's, DOMINO'S sugar. The sugar company challenged the right of the pizza maker to adopt the same name in this fashion but lost in court.

55

The Message

Most effective commercial names will consist either of common English words (such as ARROW to designate shirts, JAGUAR to designate cars) or words created by the techniques described above on page 52-53. There are several different relationships between the commercial name and the thing it designates, whether product or service or organization, which may be exploited, ranging from the name that is purely descriptive (the least desirable type) to one that is suggestive or even purely arbitrary. Generally speaking, only a coined word can be arbitrary, conveying absolutely no information, since every English word, if used to name something, will always carry with it certain connotations. Even many made-up, seemingly 'meaningless' words, furthermore, will have positive or negative (or neutral) connotations, as the example of the B.F. GOODRICH marketing test discussed below under "Testing the Product" shows. There are times when it may be appropriate to have a "neutral" name which openly suggests nothing, as in the case of naming large corporate conglomerates. In the great majority of circumstances, however, the most effective names will either be suggestive of the product or service or company line or aimed at motivating the potential buyer. Either common English words or coined words that are *not* arbitrary but carry a message (NYQUIL and SYNCHILLA [a kind of synthetic fur], for example) can be pressed into service for this purpose.

In some cases, a name that once had favorable associations has all but lost them, causing the name to appear arbitrary, whimsical to today's buyer. Certainly, one whole class of business names succeeds by this tactic: the name works precisely because it is inappropriate, weird, and it is this element of strangeness that makes the name memorable (as in the case of BICYCLE playing cards, which picture 2 Cupids riding bicycles, and KIWI shoe polish, with an illustration of a Kiwi bird on the can or bottle). While the choice of CAMEL in 1907 was at that time powerfully suggestive of the then relatively unfamiliar world of the Orient, as well as denotative of the Turkish tobaccos that comprised the cigarette product, the word has lost most—if not all—of these original associations. It has gone from being a name that invited the user to

56

experience the mystery of the East to one that seems unconnected to its product at all. It is revealing that today's ads for this brand of cigarette anthropomorphize the camel, turning it into a man in a tuxedo. The animal now becomes a symbol of a certain type of man. He is portrayed as a Los Vegas habitué, the owner of an expensive sports car, a man with beautiful women in his life, in short, a "smooth character."

In the majority of instances of common English words employed in the naming of products, the name will imply certain values which the buyer shares. The naming of automobiles, for instance, often elevates the art of implication to a new high. Some of the most effective names for cars, such as JAGUAR, symbolically suggest the realm of values which the potential buyer (male, affluent) identifies most strongly with. William Lyons, the founder of the company that manufactures Jaguars, was reputed to have compiled a list of literally hundreds of fleet-footed animals in his search for an appropriate name for his new car. Having exhaustively considered all the potential choices, he found the jaguar to be the animal most expressive of the particular attributes of his automobile. The same type of symbolism is at work for a different, but related market in the use of PUMA as a brand name for an athletic shoe or COUGAR to designate another type of automobile.

George Eastman, founder of Eastman Kodak Company, had this view on trademarks: A trademark should be (1) short, (2) vigorous, (3) incapable of being misspelled to an extent that will destroy its identity, and (4) it must mean nothing. Not everyone will agree with (4), but the other points he makes seem almost universally accepted. To this list, we would add: the name should not use hyphens, if at all avoidable. It should be easily pronounceable. It should be memorable. It should lend itself well to graphic representation. It should, of course, be legally available, Finally, it should be attractive from a design point of view.*

*Some designers have concluded that the most visually attractive business names possess a clean, horizontal sweep. The name begins with a straight-backed letter, such as E or D, and avoids *all* small letter descenders (g's, p's, q's, and y's) that fall below the line. Examples: EXXON, DIEHARD, KODAK.

The Message 1: Symbols

The use of animal or plant names to symbolize values is a very important source of commercial names that should not be overlooked. The wyvern, a type of mythic animal (a dragon) stands for diligence, for instance, the bee for industriousness, the lily for purity. Each of these animals or plants appears in pictorial form in heraldic imagery as well as in modern adaptations, both pictorial and verbal.[2] Such symbols, drawn in whole or part from the natural world, appeal to powerful, often unconscious forces, making them some of the most motivating of all images.

The Message 2: Mythological names

Mythological names also offer a rich vein of imagery which can be tapped in commercial naming. MIDAS mufflers, HELEN OF TROY cosmetics, AJAX cleanser exemplify this use of the names of mythic figures or places to personify certain values or convey information about business products or services. Midas was the mythical king of Greece, whose touch turned everything to gold. Hence the expression, "the Midas touch," connotes someone with the ability to turn everything to advantage. The name applied to mufflers is suggestive at the same time as being elusive. By contrast, the use of Helen of Troy, reputed the world's must beautiful woman, to name a cosmetics line, and Ajax, known for his brute strength, to christen a cleanser, are much more straightforward.

The Message 3: Historical names

For the financially minded, the names of mutual funds supply many examples of historical allusion which embody such values as thrift, wisdom, and steadfast devotion to principle, from the SPARTAN Money Market Fund to the FRANKLIN Group and the PURITAN Group. LINCOLN and DE SOTO cars offer further illustration of the prevalence of historical names in the business world.

The Message 4: Biblical names and Saints' names

The Bible is another excellent source of commercial names. The SAMSON CORDAGE CO., owners of the oldest trademark in America still in use, chose the biblical name of Samson as connotative of the strength of its rope. A pictorial representation of Samson

---

2   The P. Gaines Co., publisher of this book, uses the wyvern as its colophon (see the title page of this book for an example of a wyvern).

wrestling a lion supplies an accompanying logo to the name. Saints' names also figure in many trademarks and trade names today, as in ST.MARTIN'S Press and ST. MARY'S blankets, to cite but two examples.

The Message 5: Geographic names

The problem with geographic names used as business names that indicate *actual* place of origin, as already pointed out, is that they are not registrable and protectable legally unless they acquire a distinctiveness from continual use for a period of years. Many pseudo-geographic brand names, on the other hand, exploit the favorable associations connected with particular locales but have absolutely no connection with the places referred to. Many examples of successful names abound in this category, such as NEWPORT and MALIBU cigarettes, manufactured by the AMERICAN TOBACCO CO., or THE NEW YORK SPAGHETTI HOUSE (located in Cleveland). Names in this second category are immediately registrable with the PTO, provided they meet the general criteria of registration.

The Message 6: Literary names

A relatively untapped area for new names is that offered by literary allusions, names drawn from novels, plays, poems, and other works of literature. While this area tends to overlap with that of mythological allusions, in the case of the classic literature of Greece and Rome, modern literary works also can provide a field of new names. Dickens is a favorite source. How about a bridal shop called "Miss Havisham's", named after an eccentric old lady in Dickens's novel *Great Expectations* who has never taken off her wedding dress since the moment she was jilted on her wedding day years before? A bookstore in the Chicago area, for example, has adopted the name GREAT EXPECTATIONS as its commercial identifier, and PICKWICK, another Dickens' name, designates another book retailer. Such allusions will be lost on some classes of buyers, of course. If your business will be a retail store in a working class neighborhood, and your customers are plumbers, electricians, mechanics, and carpenters, you will need a name in line with the experiences and expectations of your clientele, regardless of whether or not you have a degree in English literature.

The Message 7: Puns

On the surface, puns appear to be anti-message, since they undermine the literal meaning of words. Through their humorous effects, however, they perhaps give us a deeper message. Have fun, don't take yourself too seriously they seem to say. A Massachusetts construction company named ERECTION SPECIALTIES, for example, finds that its humorous name works as an ice-breaker when its owner is soliciting new clients. A name that succeeds in giving us a laugh is often as effective as the more conventional type of commercial nomenclature.

The Message: Unintended Meanings

Unintended meanings of words can work for or against your business goals. This issue normally comes up only if you will be exporting your products to other countries, or if you will be marketing to one or more ethnic subcultures in this country. In such cases, attention must be paid to possibly unforeseen effects of names when used outside their original language. The Chinese pictograms for the sounds of the brand name COCA-COLA contain the words for "delicious" and "pleasure" in Chinese, a lucky accident in this instance. It is reported that in certain parts of Canada, BIG MACS is slang for large breasts. A brand of Swedish toilet paper termed KRÄPP, a Finnish de-icer called PISS, and a Japanese soft drink named PSCHITT are standard examples of commercial names from other cultures that definitely won't work in English. ROLLS ROYCE is reported to have axed its proposed Silver Mist trademark when it dawned on someone in the company that "mist" in German means "human fecal matter." Enco was likewise eliminated as a possible choice for the new name for Standard Oil Of New Jersey when it was found that it meant "stalled car" in Japanese. EXXON, which has no apparent meaning in any language, proved to be the final choice.

Names that evoke the product v. ones that stroke the buyer

SUNKIST and CARESS are names that evoke, but do *not* describe, the nature of the products they designate. OUT OF YOUR MIND...AND INTO THE MARKET PLACE (a business publishing company) exemplifies another type of name, which bases its appeal on the specific desires of the targeted audience. It describes every businessman's or woman's ideal progression from thought to marketable reality. This name also employs a pun that cleverly reverses the usual meaning of the expression "out of your mind" (that is, crazy), turning it into an image of a percolating brain factory.

Both of these types of marks are highly appealing for their targeted audience, although one type plays upon the desirable qualities of the goods or services themselves, while the other pitches its appeal to the mentality of a particular group of potential buyers. Both are clearly effective. Particular products or services may lend themselves better to one approach instead of another, or a combination of both. The name JAGUAR, for instance, in a careful mirroring effect, suggests both the attributes of the product *and* the ideal image of the buyer. Do not fall into the common trap of selecting a name which merely describes your product, however. Every telephone directory is replete with such unimaginative examples of Twenty-Four Hour Plumbers or Experienced Roofers.

When to use meaningless coined words

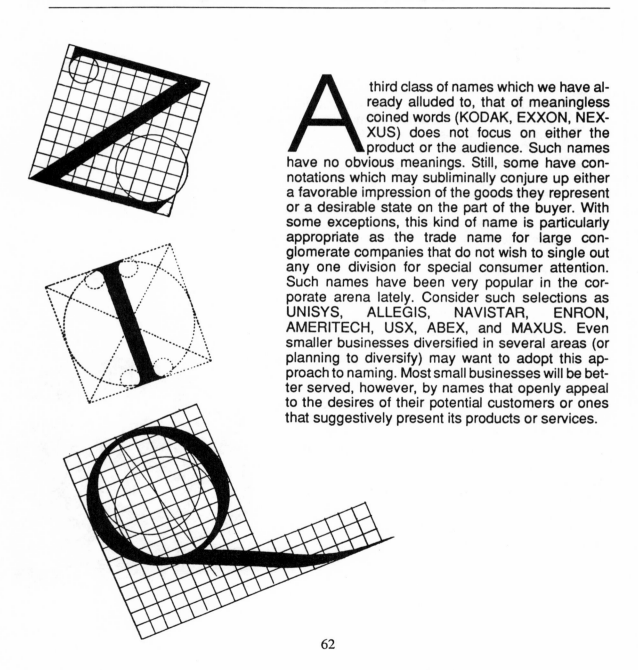

A third class of names which we have already alluded to, that of meaningless coined words (KODAK, EXXON, NEXUS) does not focus on either the product or the audience. Such names have no obvious meanings. Still, some have connotations which may subliminally conjure up either a favorable impression of the goods they represent or a desirable state on the part of the buyer. With some exceptions, this kind of name is particularly appropriate as the trade name for large conglomerate companies that do not wish to single out any one division for special consumer attention. Such names have been very popular in the corporate arena lately. Consider such selections as UNISYS, ALLEGIS, NAVISTAR, ENRON, AMERITECH, USX, ABEX, and MAXUS. Even smaller businesses diversified in several areas (or planning to diversify) may want to adopt this approach to naming. Most small businesses will be better served, however, by names that openly appeal to the desires of their potential customers or ones that suggestively present its products or services.

Formulating the message

Now that you have an overview of the types of names suitable and unsuitable for businesses, you can see that you have a number of possible routes open to you in selecting a suitable business name. We have noted that some commercial names, such as EXXON and KODAK, mean nothing in themselves. Such names acquire associations only as a result of the favorable or unfavorable behavior of the companies which they designate. Other names have meaning but one which appears incongruous and jarring—hence memorable—when placed on the particular products in question (BICYCLE playing cards, TOMATO bank). Still other names, whether common English words or new, coined words, convey important information about the product or service or company itself (Sears' DIEHARD battery, COMPAQ computer). There obviously exist different philosophies of business naming and different reasons for selecting one type of name over another, as already pointed out. The great majority of effective business names falls in the *meaningful* words category that communicate vital information, whether the words are already existing ones derived from the sources we have mentioned (history, literature, myth, animal symbolism, the Bible, ordinary English words, or foreign words) or words that have been newly invented to fit the need at hand (NYQUIL, JELL-O).

We will focus on this last category of meaningful words used as commercial names in mapping out a strategy for you to follow in your search for a suitable business identity. First, plan to invest a considerable amount of time and energy in formulating the precise *message* that you want your company or your product or service to convey. Set aside a minimum of three hours' meeting time for discussion of this matter with those involved with the business. In doing this essential mental exercise, you will need to answer such questions as: What, if anything, is unique about your business? Are its exact same products or services widely available through other suppliers? If so, what is your particular "angle"? If not, what distinguishes your products or services from those of others? Whom are you targeting as the buyer of your goods or services (be as specific as possible, identifying your customer's class status and education level and language capacities)? You should do a detailed write-up of the message about your company's identity and the nature of its goods and/or services and targeted audience in one or two pages of description covering all the relevant information. Now condense this statement into a short paragraph of four sentences, focusing on the most significant benefits your company or product provides the public. Distill the essence into one sentence. At this point, you can include only a few select features, so be sure to single out the most compelling ones. When you can extract from that sentence one word or a short phrase that captures the heart of your enterprise, you will be close to having a potential name for your business, which may be whimsical, hard-hitting, or poetic. The ideal name will crystallize in language what your business stands for.

Testing the name

Some recommend testing of potential names on consumers for their effectiveness. This is certainly a valuable source of information about your selection(s), whether you want to devise formal tests or simply try out the possible name candidates on your friends and associates. Such tests can run the gamut from a simple "like" or "dislike" evaluation of the choices in relation to a product description to much more in-depth analyses that rate the name for a number of different relevant factors.

When B.F. GOODRICH COMPANY tested proposed names for a new synthetic fiber on a group of housewives, for example, it received some very revealing responses. One of the names, "Merex," suggested to the respondents a soap in four out of ten interviews,[3] while another, "Dicuna," produced no measurable response at all, either positive or negative. "DARLAN," the name that emerged the victor, was chosen because it did, in fact, remind most of the test subjects of a luxurious synthetic fiber.

---

3   To me, it's an ant-killer. *ed. note.*

Characteristics of a good name: memorability, appeal,...

To test for the memorability of a particular name, you can read to your chosen guinea persons a list of six names (including your test name) and ask them to repeat to you as many of the names as they can recall. The higher the recall rate for your prospective choice, the more memorable.

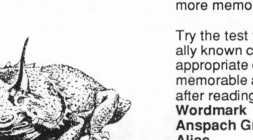

Try the test yourself. Here are names of six nationally known commercial name consultant firms. How appropriate do you find their business names? How memorable are they? Which ones stick in your mind after reading the list once?

Wordmark
Anspach Grossman Portugal
Alias
Lippincott & Margulies
NameLab
Interbrand

A simple associative test can elicit other important information about the *effect* of the prospective name—its meaning and connotations for the intended audience, whether it is irritating or appealing, drab or sensual, whether it suggests a toothpaste when, in fact, your product is a wristwatch, etc. In its most basic form, it asks the question: What do you think of when you hear the word _____ ? (*fill in the blank with the test word or phrase*).

More pointed questions which ask for an evaluation of the name in connection with the particular goods or services to be named can elicit more specific information and bring to the surface any negative elements of the name prospect. It is important that such questions only be posed to persons who actually fit the buyer profile that you have developed. If garbage collectors are your targeted market, don't waste your time asking hairdressers or bartenders their opinion. Go right to the horse's mouth.

Selected prices of name creation services or tools

☛$19.95—Price of this book[4]

☛$195—NAMER, a name creation computer program from SALINON CORP., Dallas

☛$7,500—Customized name selection for small businesses from the firm of SIEGEL & GALE

☛$30,000-50,000—Cost of naming your business, by DELANO, GOLDMAN & YOUNG

☛$150,000-$1 million—complete corporate identity creation, including logo, by LIPPINCOTT & MARGULIES

---

4   **And it's worth it!—ed.**

Part 3: Legal Considerations

The Search Is On

In Part 2 of this book, we concerned ourselves with the creative process of naming. Right now, let us look at what you should do *after* you have come up with what you consider a suitable name. It sounds right to your ear, it cleverly suggests your product line and/or appeals to the audience you want to reach, but the first thing you want to know at this point is: Is it available? Or is someone else already using the name? Approximately three-quarters of the prospective names that are subjected to a legal search turn up *unavailable* for use. Regardless of whether or not you plan to register the trademark or service mark with either the federal Patent and Trademark Office or the state, you need to be as certain as possible that the mark is clear, so you will not run the risk of being sued for trademark infringement. In the case of a trade name, although registration is not an option, you can still be sued if the trade name you select is the same as or confusingly similar to someone else's trade name, trademark, or service mark.

Below, we will consider separately the search processes involved in (1) a trademark or service mark search and (2) a company trade name search, although both these types of searches overlap.

In the instance of a trademark or service mark, you will need to search other trademarks and service marks already in existence, both registered and unregistered, as well as trade names that might represent potential areas of conflict. The PTO can refuse registration of a trademark or service mark on the grounds that it is confusingly similar to another's *trade name*. This rarely happens in reality, unless the trade name in question is very well known, since the PTO does not have the means at its disposal to search for trade name conflicts (trademark conflicts it carefully researches, however). The burden therefore falls upon the individual to determine that the proposed mark does not violate the rights of other trademark *and* trade name holders. The reverse is also true. In the case of a trade name search, you need to explore *not only* other trade names *but also* trademarks and service marks, which might be the same as or deceptively similar to your chosen mark. We have already noted that trademarks and service marks do not have to be registered to be effective, since trademark rights are conferred by first and continued use of the mark in commerce.

So, where to begin? Any search should start with the marks that *are* registered. There are about 1 million of these alone, at present. Your first concern, then, will be to uncover prior registrations and applied-for marks identical to or confusingly similar to the name you have decided on.

Trademark or service mark searching with TRADEMARKSCAN

The fastest and most efficient way to search both the existing registrations and pending marks is through two computer data bases produced by Thomson and Thomson. The first is called TRADEMARKSCAN—FEDERAL and it provides access to all active and pending trademarks on file in the U.S. Patent and Trademark Office. This file includes registered marks used on every type of product or service marketed commercially in the United States. It is updated weekly with new entries from the PTO and the *Official Gazette* and contains active marks from 1884 to the present, as well as inactive ones from 1984 to the present. The second data base, produced by the same company, is called TRADEMARKSCAN—STATE, and it provides access to all trademark registrations in the fifty states.

Each record in these two files provides the name of the trademark or service mark, the U.S. and International class of goods or services numbers, the owner's name, a description of the goods or services, and other pertinent information.

Let us assume that we conduct a search of TRADEMARKSCAN for the U.S. class of goods 038 (prints and publications) for possible conflicts with a proposed trademark for a series of business publications to be called the Gaines Hotline. We find in our search a number of similar marks and two exact matches of the word Gaines in this class of goods. We reprint below one of these two "hits" in its entirety to show the information provided.

```
8/2/4      (Item 4 from file: 226)
           03045839
GAINES DOG RESEARCH CENTER       and Design
       US CLASS   : *038 *(Prints and Publications)
       INTL CLASS : *016 *(Paper Goods and Printed Matter)
       STATUS : Cancelled   REG. NO. : 1077362
       REG. DATE : November 15, 1977
       CAN. DATE : April 10, 1984
       PUBLISHED : August 23, 1977
       GOODS/SERVICES : PERIODICAL PAMPHLETS FOR VETERINARIANS, BREEDERS
           AND FANCIERS
       CANCELLATION SEC : 8
       SERIES CODE : 73  SERIAL NO. : 045839
       FILED : March 05, 1975
       DATE OF FIRST USE : December, 1968
       ORIGINAL OWNER : GENERAL FOODS CORPORATION, WHITE PLAINS, N.Y.
       CLAIMS : THE DESCRIPTIVE WORDS "DOG RESEARCH CENTER" ARE
           DISCLAIMED APART FROM THE MARK AS A WHOLE.*
       DESIGN PHRASE : TWO OVALS ONE WITH LETTERING AND ONE WITH PICTURE
           OF DOG SITTING
```

As the print-out tells us, Gaines Dog Research Center was the name of a registered trademark denoting a publication about animal nutrition put out by GENERAL FOODS CORPORATION. We also learn that the mark was cancelled on April 10, 1984, evidently because an affidavit of continued use was not filed with the PTO during the sixth year following the date of registration (November 15, 1977).

Let us assume that we also decide to search the related class of Advertising and Business Services (U.S. class 101) for possible conflicting marks. None of the marks which the computer picks up appears similar enough to cause concern, but several of these graphically illustrate how similar sounding words and words that are not in the first position of the name are uncovered by the computer search. For example,

The Outlook Resort Boutique at Gainey Ranch
Royce Gaines' Carpet Pro's of Frankfort
The One and A-Half Gainer Club

all represent registered marks which have "Gaines" or a similar word as a part of them. Notice that this key word, furthermore, is embedded in the mark in such a way that a manual alphabetical search of a printed trademark directory might not be able to detect it, since you are usually limited to looking for the *first* word of the mark in a manual search (some alphabetical directories, however, will highlight key words—see below).

Although the proposed trademark has two key words, "Gaines" and "hotline," we are assuming that the very prevalence of the use of the word "hotline" precludes trademark protection. If there did happen to already be a registered trademark termed "Gaines Hotline" in the same class of goods as our proposed one, then this would, of course, bar our adoption of this mark. However, our search of the key word "Gaines" would uncover all usages of that term for the particular class of goods in question, including a "Gaines Hotline" if one indeed existed as a trademark registration or applied-for mark.

The other consideration is a deceptively similar mark but not an exact match, for example, a GAINS HOTLINE, or a GAIN HOTLINE. If either of these trademarks already existed for a business publication, our proposed one would be too similar and would have to be discarded. It is possible to search for these similar sounding but differently spelled names as well. TRADEMARKSCAN is also equipped with the capacity to search homophones (words with the same or very similar sound but different meanings and spellings, such as "heir" and "air"), since these present areas of potential trademark conflict as well.

In addition to searching for variant spellings of the same word, which are regarded as exact equivalents by the PTO—a search for CLEAN will select marks containing KLEAN, CLEEN, and KLEEN, for example—other problem areas, such as foreign language equivalents and numbers, whether written as Roman or Arabic numberals or words, are also easily handled by TRADEMARKSCAN. No manual search can match the computer's ability to find, homophones, numbers, embedded words, and foreign equivalents.

The two TRADEMARKSCAN data bases are available on-line through DIALOG Information Services. If you subscribe to DIALOG, you can do the search yourself, currently at a rate of $125.00 per hour, plus .85 for each record printed out. Many larger public libraries now offer DIALOG as well.

The P. Gaines Co. now offers a complete computer search service. Our skilled operators will search your trade name, trademark, or service mark in TRADEMARKSCAN—FEDERAL as well as in TRADEMARKSCAN—STATE for one low fee. Write for our free brochure describing this service (see the order form in the back of this book).

Trademark Directories

See Appendix B for sample pages from the directories mentioned in this section.

There also exist directories listing registered trademarks which are available at many law libraries and larger public libraries. GALE RESEARCH publishes *Brands and Their Companies*. This book is primarily an alphabetical compilation of trademarks (brand names) and service marks, and includes some certification marks as well. The Government Printing Office weekly puts out the *Official Gazette* of the Patent and Trademark Office. The trademark section of this publication lists new trademark registrations, as well as trademarks published for opposition, and canceled, amended, and renewed registrations. As noted previously, new registrations appear on either of two registers in the *Official Gazette*, the Principal or the Supplemental Register. The PTO also publishes two related directories: (1) the *Index to Trademarks Registered with the U.S. Patent and Trademark Office*, a compilation, arranged according to **company name**, of all the trademarks registered and renewed in the previous year; (2) the *Index to Trademark and Service Classes*, an alphabetical locator of the classification number of goods and services. If the product name you are investigating is one for washing machines, for instance, a check under this entry would give you the class number for washing machines. This index is only available at Patent Depository Libraries, however. The following commercially published directory provides a similar index to determine class number.

The Trademark Register, published annually by a patent and trademark searching service in Washington, D.C., provides a listing of every active registered mark in existence. The major drawback to this guide is that it does not have a merged alphabetical listing for all classes of trademark classifications. Rather, each mark is assigned to its class

75

of goods or services and the marks in each class are then alphabetically presented. One must first determine what class(es) to look under for a given mark (a subject index, as noted, is included for this purpose), and then consult two sections of classifications—pre-1974 marks are registered under the U.S. numbering system in one section and those issued after 1974 appear under their International classification number in a second section. To make matters more complicated, only basic information is included for each mark: the name itself, the class number(s), the date it was published in the *Official Gazette*, and the registration number. The mark must then be looked up in the appropriate issue of the *Official Gazette* if more detailed information is needed.

COMPU-MARK also publishes its annual multi-volume trademark index, the *Compu-Mark Directory of U.S. Trademarks.* It, too, lists trademarks alphabetically within each class (according to the international classification system). All key words in a multi-word name appear in the index, not just the first important word. Marks that have been applied for but not yet registered on either the Principal or Supplemental Registers are also included in its listings. COMPU-MARK also makes its data available online to subscribers as well as in printed form.

Trademark searching— *Shepard's U.S. Patents and Trademarks Citations*

This directory, published by McGraw-Hill, will only be available at law libraries and a few large public libraries, but it can be invaluable if you can get your hands on a copy. Look up your proposed trademark or service mark in it and see if you find a similar or the exact name. The entries under each name refer to mentions of that trademark in legal publications. By going to the articles cited, you can trace the history of litigation surrounding a particular mark. The fact that there have occurred legal suits over a given mark should alert you to the fact that a particular company is willing to aggressively contest any challenges to its rights in that name. In such a case, it may be folly to select the same or a very similar name. The in-depth coverage of trademark lawsuits provided by these citations offers a fascinating and invaluable tool for the serious trademark searcher.

An interesting case involving the names "Gaines" is cited. GENERAL FOODS CORPORATION, registrant of GAINES DOG MEAL and other uses of GAINES to denote dog food, filed suit against James O. Gaines, who sought to register the trademark GAINES for a type of cleanser. There was no question that the dog food makers were the first to use the name, but the preliminary ruling by the examiner was in favor of the cleanser manufacturer, who found the two products so dissimilar in characteristics, use, and sales appeal that no confusion should arise to cause the public to assume that the products emanated from a single source. Upon appeal, this decision was reversed, however, when it was brought out that the cleanser maker was using the logo of a dog in connection with the trademark of GAINES. Since the picture of the dog had absolutely no connection with the nature of the product, it was felt that the complete trademark, consisting of the name and logo, would cause buyers unconsciously to see some connection between the two products. The existence of the dog picture in this case tipped the scales. This example shows how a logo may play a decisive role in the legal acceptablility or non-acceptability of a given mark.

Trademark searching—Other Sources

We have noted that trademark rights are conferred by usage, and marks do not have to be registered in order to be effective. Your search should definitely not stop, therefore, with TRADEMARKSCAN. If the search of the federal and state registrations and applied-for marks does not turn up any potential conflicts, your next major concern will be to uncover prior users who have *not* registered their marks with either the Patent and Trademark Office or any state government's trademark division. Generally speaking, the larger and more profitable companies who have trademarks in use will have gone through the procedure of registration on the federal or the state and federal levels. Frequently, these trademarks will serve a dual purpose as both trademark and trade name for a given company.

Many smaller companies will not have registered their trademarks, however, and their corresponding trade names will not be well known. The purpose of this extended search is to discover both these unregistered marks (sometimes referred to in common parlance as "common law trademarks") as well as trade names that might conflict with your proposed trademark.

We recommend the following procedures in addition to a computer search of registered trademarks.

Trademark searching—Trade directories, etc.

(1) Industry and trade directories should be manually searched. No matter what field your new or already going business is in, your local public library should either have on hand or be able to get for you trade directories in your field of expertise. If you were checking a trademark which you were considering for a new drug, the first product developed by your small pharmaceutical firm, you would need to examine such standard trade sources for potential conflicts as:

•The Physician's Desk Reference (prescription, nonprescription, ophthalmic, and radiologic editions)
•The Merck Index
•Trademarks Listed with the Pharmaceutical Manufacturers Association
•American Drug Index
•USAN and the USP Dictionary of Drug Names

The standard reference directories in each field will, of course, be different—A reference librarian can guide you to the works essential to consult in a given industry, from medicine to chicken farming.

(2) Telephone directories provide another important source of information about businesses. At present, larger public libraries have phone directories in their reference departments from all major U.S. cities. Plan to spend an afternoon in the library searching phone books for the same or confusingly similar *trade names* as the trademark or service mark that you have selected.

(3) Computer data bases. The Electronic Yellow Pages provides the names and addresses of some 4 million businesses. It is an excellent source of trade names. It is also possible to search trademark *owners*, that is, trade names, in the TRADEMARKSCAN data base. THE TRINET COMPANY data base also has an extensive listing of company names.

business will have to have attained at least a small measure of success in order to be a member of a professional organization, to have a telephone listing, or to appear in the Electronic Yellow Pages (DUN & BRADSTREET-rated businesses), TRADEMARKSCAN, or TRINET. These are the major sources of information for detecting existing business names which might conflict with the one chosen for your business. The section below on Searching Company Trade Names provides additional sources of information on company trade names that can be manually searched. If you search all these sources and find no potential problems, you will have good justification for believing that your name is clear and available.

The "Z" factor

There always exists the chance that some other company that is too small to appear in any of these directories or data bases has adopted the very same name that you now cherish as your own. We refer to this possibility as the "Z factor," that element of uncertainty, however small, which cannot be eliminated. Those who want to reduce the Z factor to the greatest extent possible can do so by leaving no stone unturned, ferreting out every source of information on products, services, or manufacturers in their particular field of interest, as well as trade names in every field. Such thoroughness will give you the best possible assurances of a problem-free name. Whatever approach you adopt, whether the fine-tooth-comb search or just the basics, ma'm, keep in mind two, apparently contradictory, facts: (1) A conscientious search is essential for clearance. (2) No system of checking is absolutely fool-proof, and some element of uncertainty will always remain. One can worry oneself to death about this possibility, or accept it good-naturedly as the price of doing business in the real world. If you have done a competent search, or had an attorney do one for you, you have the added assurance of knowing that a company too small to show up in any of your investigations is, in all likelihood, not going to be in a position to take you to court over trademark or trade name infringement. There are no guarantees in this realm, however—only educated guesses.

Searching a company trade name

(1) The first step in assuring the legality of your use of a specific trade name to designate your business is dictated by your state incorporation laws. No state will let you do business under a name that someone else has already incorporated under in that particular state. In addition, many larger companies incorporate in one state (New York, for example), but do business in many other states as well. Such businesses are required by law to register as "foreign corporations" in *all* the other states in which they do business. Your chosen name cannot be the same as or deceptively similar to the names of any of these foreign corporations doing business in your state either.

Every state has procedures whereby you can check your proposed business name against a list of names of both the domestic and foreign corporations with a legal and business presence in your state. In Illinois, for example, a directory of such names, called the *Illinois Certified List*, is published by the Secretary of State. Larger public libraries in the state will have this list available for your inspection. In addition, in Illinois you can phone the Secretary of State's Office for a check of availability of a particular name, at (217) 982-9520 or 9521 in Springfield.

(2) Examine as many telephone directories in your state as possible (ideally all of them) for business names that are the same as or very similar to yours. Again, larger public libraries will have a complete set of state phone books for your use. The telephone directory check may uncover businesses that have not incorporated but that are doing business under the name you wish to use. Legally, from the state's point of view (with the exception of California and New York), you are free to adopt the very same name as someone else's unincorporated business if you wish, in spite of the fact that you may be infringing upon someone else's trade name or trademark. In other words, the state leaves it entirely up to the individual business owner to take action against you if you are violating his or her trademark rights. Although you may not have to worry about trademark litigation arising from these small, unincorporated businesses at present, you need to ask yourself if you really want to do business under a name that someone in the state is already using. At some point in the future, furthermore, that small business may be considerably larger and decide to aggressively defend its trademark rights. In such a case, your name choice may very well prove to be a legal liability.

(3) Consult telephone directories and industry directories at the library for listings of company names in other states. If you find other businesses in the same or a related field using the same or a very similar name as yours, you may want to reconsider your choice, especially if you plan to be involved in interstate commerce and will likely be dealing with the same customers as the already established business(es). Some standard reference sources for business names, listed alphabetically and/or by industry include:

Dun's Business Information Services
 (on microfiche)
This is an alphabetical listing of the some 6 million U.S. businesses that DUN and BRADSTREET has financial information about. A check of this listing will be a good indication if you have picked a name that is very common and used by many other companies or a distinctive moniker. While you may choose to use a trade name that is already in use in another state and escape detection, you may also, as noted, eventually be sued for trademark infringement, regardless of whether the name functions solely as a company trade name or plays a dual role as both trade name and trademark or service mark. That is why, in step (4) below, a trademark search of the name is highly recommended as well. If both businesses are in the same or a related field, by all means avoid the temptation to adopt the same name.

Standard and Poor's Register of Corporations
This directory lists some 45,000 names of U.S. corporations and their addresses and phone numbers, as well as the names of company directors and executives.

In addition to general corporate directories, there also exists a large selection of directories covering individual industries, such as: *Corporate Technology Directory* (high-tech industries), *Data Sources* (computer hardware and software companies), *Dun's Industrial Guide* (metalworking industry), *Directory of American Research and Technology* (corporate research facilities), *Post's Pulp and Paper Directory* (paper industry), *Sheldon's Retail* (chain stores), *Standard Directory of Advertisers* (major advertisers), *Thomas Grocery Register* (food products *and services), Who's Who in Electronics* (electronics manufacturers and distributors). There are also state manufacturing directories available for each of the 50 states.

Searching a Company Trade Name (Continued)

Million Dollar Directory
Another DUN and BRADSTREET information source, this directory supplies an alphabetical listing of some 160,000 company names, with addresses. It has a breakdown of names by industry.

Thomas Register of American Manufacturers
This directory lists 135,000 manufacturing company names by industry. It also contains a trademark section, which lists both registered and unregistered trademarks. While it does not hurt to look at this list, it contains only a fraction of the trademarks and service marks available through the data base TRADEMARKSCAN. A similar guide, *Macrae's Blue Book,* also covers the manufacturing sector, with some 50,000 company listings.

Ward's Business Directories
This 3-volume reference work features 110,000 publicly- and privately-held U.S. corporations, as well as 15,000 foreign corporations.

Directories in Print
This GALE RESEARCH publication is an annotated guide to over 10,000 business and industrial directories, professional and scientific rosters, and directory data bases. It can assist you in finding specialized industry directories.

Summary: In order to do business in your particular state, you are only *required* to follow the procedure outlined in step (1). Clearance of your company name by the corporation division of your state is no guarantee of trademark clearance, however. You can be given the green light to use a given name by the state and still find yourself embroiled in costly trademark litigation.

To repeat, when a state grants permission to incorporate under a specific name, it is not making any judgment as to the legality of the name itself. Its "clearance" merely indicates that the name does not conflict with the name of any other domestic or foreign corporation doing business in that state. (It does not even consider whether the name is the same as or deceptively similar to sole proprietors and partnerships currently operating in the state.) Although trade names are not registrable with the PTO, they are *still* legally protected in the same way as trademarks against unfair competition. Through the use of a particular company name in commerce, a business symbolizes its reputation. For someone else to then assume that name and to profit from the goodwill that another has accrued is clearly illegal.

Searching a Company Trade Name (Continued)

R**emember, too,** that many company trade names can serve a dual role as trademarks or service marks as well as business names. Because of this ambiguity which allows one name to function in two capacities, your company name may infringe upon someone else's registered or unregistered trademark. This is particularly a problem if (1) your business is in a related field as the trademark or service mark or if (2) the mark is owned by a large, powerful company that will prosecute *all* perceived trademark infringements. Obviously, no newcomer nowadays can designate his business, not to mention his products or services, with such names as KODAK, EXXON, or MCDONALD'S, even if one's name happens to be Old McDonald. These particular companies have legions of aggressive attorneys to back up their "strong" trademarks and trade names, who are ready to stifle any hint of dilution of their marks.

(4) Ideally, you should have a computer search of TRADEMARKSCAN in *all* classes of goods and services to look for conflicts with your proposed company trade name. This will prove expensive, however. If you carefully avoid any names which might conflict with major brands or service marks *in any field* and search the same class(es) of goods and services as your own, this will provide reasonable assurance of good faith compliance with trademark law. Say that you will be manufacturing fine wood furniture and have chosen to do business under the name of Willoughby Enterprises. When you search the appropriate class, if you find a trademark "Willoughby" for a line of furniture, you had better reconsider your name choice, since an apparent conflict is clearly evident.

Exceptions: Trade names which are not protectable

Although we have said that trade names are ordinarily protectable under common law in the same manner as trademarks, the same criteria that would make a trademark unregistrable (and hence unprotectable) would also render a trade name unprotectable. If the name is generic, that is, merely descriptive of the goods or services provided by the company (Experienced Roofers, for example), or based on the surname of the owner (Smith's Dry Cleaners), it is not protectable *unless* it has acquired such distinctiveness over a period of time as to be identified as the *sole* supplier of such goods and/or services. This will never happen, of course, in 99 out of 100 such cases. The name itself in a sense has already saddled the owner with a local, as opposed to a national, mentality and market presence. For the timid of heart, the selection of a *deliberately generic* trade name or a personal surname (provided that there is not already a dominant

business operating under that same name) is one solution to the naming dilemma. You don't ordinarily have to worry about someone else suing you over a name that is not legally protectable to begin with! Just as "safe" names tend to mire their owners in low expectations, so too do more adventuresome names pose greater risks as well as greater rewards.

What to look for

We offer the following general preliminary guidelines for doing either manual or computer searches for trademarks, service marks, or trade names.

(1) In the case of trademarks, identical matches of your name with an already existing name for the same class of goods (say, a name for a dental drill in international class number 10) automatically rule out that particular name choice in most circumstances. On the other hand, if you are searching for a trade name's clearance, an existing trademark in *any* class of goods that is identical with your potential trade name must be taken into consideration. As a rule of thumb, the larger the company that owns the rights to a given mark, the stronger the likelihood of legal problems if you adopt the same or a very similar name for your company trade name.

Of course, some words, such as "elite," "premier," "imperial," "royal," or "paramount" appear as part of a trademark in virtually every class of goods. The very frequency of the presence of such terms makes them exceedingly 'weak' marks indeed, which means that you can probably use them also. Elite Gallery is a safe choice but not a very distinctive one as the name of a gift shop. You can assume that its very frequency of use makes it available to virtually anyone without fear of claims of infringement. If indeed you care whether there exist other Elite Galleries, a search might be advisable. In all likelihood, there probably are dozens of stores with this exact name in the United States.

If you add yours to the list, you are opting for a name with no originality which you are sharing with a host of others. If you adopt such a name and are yourself eminently successful, you will have little or no protection against opportunists who may decide to capitalize on your good fortune and open similar businesses under the same name.

(2) Do not be misled by spelling variants, run-on words, and other apparent differences. The Patent and Trademark Office does *not* take these elements into account in weighing whether marks are conflictive. Kwik-Cleen and Quick Clean are, for their purposes, identical marks.

(3) Marks that are *almost* the same for the same class of goods will ordinarily not be acceptable. OLD FORESTER and OLD FOSTER to designate two brands of liquor were deemed to be too close to be acceptable by the PTO. To cite another example, in the case of bicycles, ROADWAY and ROAD-MASTER were also judged to be too similar. This decision does not necessarily rule out all other uses of "road" to designate bicycles, but it shows that great care in the choice of a name utilizing that word will be required of other users to achieve distinctiveness.

(4) Words from foreign languages that, translated, mean the same as an already existing mark in the same or a related class of goods will not be allowed. CORONA, for example, is a brand of typewriter. Since the word means "crown" in Latin, the name "Crown" would not be allowable as a mark for another brand of typewriter.

Caution: Always keep clearly in mind who your competitors are and the commercial names which they employ. Avoid at all costs imitating or parodying them. If a major competitor is operating under the name of Potato Graphics, do not give in to the temptation to designate yourself as French Fry Design. Choose a name that goes in a completely different direction from those in your field, to escape claims of infringement from those most likely to raise such charges in the first place.

Caution: Avoid words that are difficult to pronounce. They will also be hard to remember.

Should you use a trademark lawyer?

(Read the fine print)

For those who can afford an attorney specializing in the field of trademarks to handle the legal aspect of their name selection and the filing and prosecution of their trademark application, this is usually a good investment, since you will be employing an expert in the field. You can, of course, do your own name search and file and defend your own trademark application if you so desire, without legal help. Or, since the PTO cannot advise prospective trademark applicants of the availability of a particular mark prior to the filing of an application, you may choose to have a search company or an attorney perform a name search but file your own application. Larger companies that plan to invest millions of dollars in a name through advertising and other types of promotion always use the services of a trademark attorney, of course, for name clearance. For the smaller company, it will depend entirely on its needs and what it can afford. The local chapter of the American Bar Association can refer you to lawyers in this particular area. If you must do the work yourself, however, plan to become knowledgeable enough to make informed decisions. Start by reading, in addition to this book, as many of the other publications listed in the bibliography as possible.

Companies already in business and operating under a problematic name

Should only those who are now in the process of going into business and actively looking for a suitable name or mark concern themselves with the business of naming? Absolutely not. Companies already in business for a few months or even for many years who selected a name or mark without full consideration of the legal and/or aesthetic ramifications of their choice should carefully examine it to see if it is the best selection that can be made. That which is haphazardly done is rarely effective. Businesses also change through diversification, mergers and acquisitions, or specialization, so that a name that once seemed suitable may now appear inappropriate. When Burger Queen decided to develop a broader menu not limited to burgers, for example, it changed its name to DRUTHER'S. When ALLIED CHEMICAL CORPORATION (now ALLIED CORPORATION) and TAMPAX INCORPORATED (now TAMBRANDS) diversified into other areas, their new names both registered their broader focus and maintained continuity with the past.

A lawsuit may also be the occasion of a name change, as in the case of the former AUTO SHACK, which changed its name to AUTOZONE after an infringement suit filed by RADIO SHACK.

After objectively weighing the current value of your trade name or mark, you can either (1) confirm that you have the best possible name or (2) recognize that a name change is in order. The longer you delay such an evaluation, the more painful the moment of truth may prove to be, particularly in the case of commercial names that were selected without any attention to the legal ramifications. Consider the hypothetical case of a clothing retailer named "Apricots" which, over the years, had grown from a small local retailer to a national chain with record sales. Recently, it had to surrender its name because of a trademark conflict, in existence from the beginning, that it failed to investigate. Today, its stores bear the name of "Plums." One wonders if, in a few years more, the "Plums" signs will also disappear, to be replaced by yet another identifier ("Plums" today, "Persimmons" tomorrow?). Even if the name had been researched in the early years of business, if not before the business was started, this problem could likely have been avoided. There is nothing more demoralizing to a mature business than to have to give up the name it has worked for years to invest with value and goodwill.

APPENDIX A

International Schedule of Classes of Goods and Services

Goods

1 Chemical products used in industry, science, photography, agriculture, horticulture, forestry; artificial and synthetic resins; plastics in the form of powders, liquids or pastes, for industrial use; manures (natural and artificial); fire extinguishing compositions; tempering substances and chemical preparations for soldering; chemical substances for preserving foodstuffs; tanning substances; adhesive substances used in industry.

2 Paints, varnishes, lacquers; preservatives against rust and against deterioration of wood; coloring matters, dyestuffs; mordants; natural resins; metals in foil and powder form for painters and decorators.

3 Bleaching preparations and other substances for laundry use; cleaning, polishing, scouring and abrasive preparations; soaps; perfumery, essential oils, cosmetics, hair lotions; dentifrices.

4 Industrial oils and greases (other than oils and fats and essential oils); lubricants; dust laying and absorbing compositions; fuels (including motor spirit) and illuminants; candles, tapers, night lights and wicks.

5 Pharmaceutical, veterinary, and sanitary substances; infants' and invalids' foods; plasters, material for bandaging; material for stopping teeth, dental wax, disinfectants; preparations for killing weeds and destroying vermin.

6 Unwrought and partly wrought common metals and their alloys; anchors, anvils, bells, rolled and cast building materials; rails and other metallic materials for railway tracks; chains (except driving chains for vehicles); cables and wires (nonelectric); locksmiths' work; metallic pipes and tubes; safes and cash boxes; steel balls; horseshoes; nails and screws; other goods in nonprecious metal not included in other classes; ores.

7 Machines and machine tools; motors (except for land vehicles); machine couplings and belting (except for land vehicles); large size agricultural implements; incubators.

8 Hand tools and instruments; cutlery, forks, and spoons; side arms.

9 Scientific, nautical, surveying and electrical apparatus and instruments (including wireless), photographic, cinematographic, optical, weighing, measuring, signalling, checking (supervision), lifesaving and teaching apparatus and instruments; coin or counterfreed apparatus; talking machines; cash registers; calculating machines; fire extinguishing apparatus.

10 Surgical, medical, dental, and veterinary instruments and apparatus (including artificial limbs, eyes and teeth).

11 Installations for lighting, heating, steam generating, cooking, refrigerating, drying, ventilating, water supply, and sanitary purposes.

12 Vehicles; apparatus for locomotion by land, air or water.

13 Firearms; ammunition and projectiles; explosive substances; fireworks.

14 Precious metals and their alloys and goods in precious metals or coated therewith (except cutlery, forks and spoons); jewelry, precious stones, horological and other chronometric instruments.

15 Musical instruments (other than ·talking machines and wireless apparatus).

16 Paper and paper articles, cardboard and cardboard articles; printed matter, newspaper and periodicals, books; bookbinding material; photographs; stationery, adhesive materials (stationery); artists' materials; paint brushes; typewriters and office requisites (other than furniture); instructional and teaching material (other than apparatus); playing cards; printers' type and cliches (stereotype).

17 Gutta percha, india rubber; balata and substitutes, articles made from these substances and not included in other classes; plastics in the form of sheets, blocks and rods, being for use in manufacture; materials for packing, stopping or insulating;

asbestos, mica and their products; hose pipes (non-metallic).

18 Leather and imitations of leather, and articles made from these materials and not included in other classes; skins, hides; trunks and travelling bags; umbrellas, parasols and walking sticks; whips, harness and saddlery.

19 Building materials, natural and artificial stone, cement, lime, mortar, plaster and gravel; pipes of earthenware or cement; roadmaking materials; asphalt, pitch and bitumen; portable buildings; stone monuments; chimney pots.

20 Furniture, mirrors, picture frames; articles (not included in other classes) of wood, cork, reeds, cane, wicker, horn, bone, ivory, whalebone, shell, amber, mother-of-pearl, meerschaum, celluloid, substitutes for all these materials, or of plastics.

21 Small domestic utensils and containers (not of precious metals, or coated therewith); combs and sponges; brushes (other than paint brushes); brush-making materials; instruments and material for cleaning purposes, steel wool; unworked or semi-worked glass (excluding glass used in building); glassware, porcelain and earthenware, not included in other classes.

22 Ropes, string, nets, tents, awnings, tarpaulins, sails, sacks; padding and stuffing materials (hair, kapok, feathers, seaweed, etc.); raw fibrous textile materials.

23 Yarns, threads.

24 Tissues (piece goods); bed and table covers; textile articles not included in other classes.

25 Clothing, including boots, shoes and slippers.

26 Lace and embroidery, ribands and braid; buttons, press buttons, hooks and eyes, pins and needles; artificial flowers.

27 Carpets, rugs, mats and matting; linoleums and other materials for covering existing floors; wall hangings (nontextile).

28 Games and playthings; gymnastic and sporting articles (except clothing); ornaments and decorations for Christmas trees.

29 Meats, fish, poultry and game; meat extracts; preserved, dried and cooked fruits and vegetables; jellies, jams; eggs, milk and other dairy products; edible oils and fats; preserves, pickles.

30 Coffee, tea, cocoa, sugar, rice, tapioca, sago, coffee substitutes; flour, and preparations made from cereals; bread, biscuits, cakes, pastry and confectionery; ices; honey, treacle; yeast, baking powder, salt, mustard, pepper, vinegar, sauces, spices; ice.

31 Agricultural, horticultural and forestry products and grains not included in other classes; living animals; fresh fruits and vegetables; seeds; live plants and flowers; foodstuffs for animals, malt.

32 Beer, ale, and porter; mineral and aerated waters and other nonalcoholic drinks; syrups and other preparations for making beverages.

33 Wines, spirits and liqueurs.

34 Tobacco, raw or manufactured; smokers' articles; matches.

Services

35 Advertising and business.

36 Insurance and financial.

37 Construction and repair.

38 Communications.

39 Transportation and storage.

40 Material treatment.

41 Education and entertainment.

42 Miscellaneous.

APPENDIX B

Sample Pages from Trademark Directories
(see pages 75-76 for a detailed description of each directory)

Brands and Their Companies

Official Gazette

The Trademark Register

The Compu-Mark Directory of U.S. Trademarks

Brands and Their Companies. **Brand name listings**

MY SWEET MERMAID

MY BEAUTIFUL SWAN - Stuffed animal, now out of production - Commonwealth Toy & Novelty Co. Inc.
MY BELL - Product description unknown - Tamura Electronic Corp. USA - JCK
MY BELOVED - Bras, girdles, now out of production - Winconia (Boston) Inc. - CBL
MY BEST FRIEND - Doll - Eugene Doll & Novelty Co. Inc.
MY BIKE - Bicycles, now out of production - Huffy Corp.
MY BOTTLE BABY - Doll, now out of production - CBS Toys
MY BRA - Bras - True Form Foundations - CBL
MY BUDDY - Candy bar - Tom's Foods Ltd.
MY BUDDY - Pet products - My Buddy - PSM
MY BUDDY - Swimming trainers - Ero Industries Inc.
MY BUDDY - Tobacco products - Sterling Tobacco Co. - TIBG
MY BUDDY - Toolboxes - The Disston Co. - BSN
MY BUDDY - Toy vehicles, dolls, plush toys - Buddy L Corp.
MY CAFE - Coffee grinder/maker, now out of production - Toshiba America Inc. [Consumer Products Business Sector]
MY CAT-ALOG - Pet products - Inky Dinky Inc. - PD
MY CHAIR - Portable infants' seats - Pansy Ellen Products Inc.
MY CHATTY PATTY - Doll and accessories - Mattel Inc. - GAZ
MY CHILD - Cosmetics for children, now out of production - Cosrich Inc.
MY CHILD - Doll and accessories - Mattel Inc.
MY CHILD - Footwear - Mercury International Trading Corp. - FND
MY CHINESE UNCLE - Footwear - Stonebridge Trading Co. - FND
MY CHOICE - Carpet, now out of production - Stevens Carpet - FLD
MY CHRISTMAS BABY - Doll - Eugene Doll & Novelty Co. Inc.
MY CHURCH TEACHES - Children's doctrinal books - Southern Publishing Association
MY CLASSIC PIZZA - The Pillsbury Co.
MY COLOR 2 - Carpet - Royalweve Carpet Mills
MY COMB & CARE BABY - Doll, now out of production - Fisher-Price Toys
MY-CORT - Eardrops, nasal spray, ophthalmic ointment - Scrip-Physician Supply Co. - DRB
MY DARLING - Flatware, now out of production - Lifetime Cutlery Corp.
MY DISH - Pet-feeding dishes - Penn-Plax Plastics Inc. - PD
MY DOGGIE'S BAG - Dog treats - Pet Life Foods Inc.
MY DOLLY - Doll accessories - Imperial Toy Corp.
MY DREAM - Eau de toilette - Goubaud - DRB
MY EPIL - Depilatory - Bache, Ella - DRB
MY EYES - Optical products - Universal Univis Inc.
MY FACE - Lipstick, powder, soap - Avon Products Inc. - SCC
MY FAIR LADY - Occasional furniture - Pulaski Furniture Corp.
MY FAIR LADY IX - Wallcoverings - Lennon Wallpaper Co. - PWD
MY FANCY - Bath powder, cologne, perfume, etc. - Miahati Inc. - DRB
MY FANCY - Optical products - Zyloware Corp.
MY FANTASY - Carpets and rugs - Patcraft Mills Inc.
MY FATHER'S BEST - Pizza - Nation Pizza Products Inc. - QFF
MY-FAVORITE - Carbon paper - Eaton Allen Ko-Rec-Type Corp. - WPS
MY FAVORITE - Ice cream - Dunkirk Ice Cream
MY FAVORITE FANTASY - Bras - Vanity Fair Mills Inc.
MY FAVORITE PEN - Tops Pen Co.
MY FAVORITE SHOES - Footwear - Benchmark Shoes Ltd. - FND
MY FAVORITE THINGS - Christmas-ornament kits - The Cracker Box Inc.
MY FAVORITE THINGS - Craft kits - Blumenthal & Co. Inc., B.
MY FEET ARE HEADED FOR... - Children's footwear - Vision Imports Inc.
MY FINANCES - Record books - Boorum & Pease Co. - OP
MY FIRST ANIMAL BOOK - Learning aids, now out of production - Texas Instruments Inc.
MY FIRST BABY DOLL - Now out of production - Fun World Inc.
MY FIRST BARBIE - Doll and accessories - Mattel Inc.
MY FIRST BEAR - Toy bear, now out of production - Those Characters From Cleveland Inc. - THC
MY FIRST BRA - Girls' bras - Teenform Inc.
MY FIRST BUDDYS - Toys - Buddy L Corp.
MY FIRST CAMERA - Eastman Kodak Co.
MY FIRST CRAYON - Writing products - Dixon Ticonderoga Co. - WIMA
MY FIRST ELECTRIC CAR - Riding toy - Combi Industries Inc. - THC
MY FIRST ELECTRIC TRIKE - Riding toy - Combi Industries Inc.
MY FIRST GAME - CBS Toys
MY FIRST INLAY - Puzzles - Bradley Co., Milton
MY FIRST MARKER - Writing products - Dixon Ticonderoga Co. - WIMA
MY FIRST PENCIL - Writing products - Dixon Ticonderoga Co.
MY FIRST PONY - Rocking horse - Sun Products Corp. [playthings]
MY FIRST PUPPY - Toy puppy, now out of production - Those Characters From Cleveland Inc. - THC
MY FOLLY - Cologne, perfume, toilet water - Parfums Duvelle Inc. - DRB
MY FOOTBALL MONSTER - Plush toy, now out of production - Those Characters From Cleveland Inc.
MY FRIEND - Doll, now out of production - Fisher-Price Toys
MY FRIEND JENNY - Doll, now out of production - Fisher-Price Toys

MY FRIEND MANDY - Doll, now out of production - Fisher-Price Toys
MY GIRL - Optical products - Art-Craft Optical Co.
MY GOODNESS - Candy - Eddyleon Chocolate Co. Inc.
MY GRANDMA'S RECIPE - Meatball-seasoning mix - Roncini, L. M.
MY GRANDMOTHER'S HOUSE - Wallcoverings - The Glidden Co.
MY GRASS - Outdoor-indoor carpets and rugs - General Felt Industries Inc. - FLD
MY HEART - Pencils, now out of production - Dakin Inc.
MY HOUSE - Children's dinnerware - Anacapa Corp.
MY ISLANDS - Cologne - The Gillette Co. - TGR
MY-K - Nasal spray, now out of production - Pharmaceutical Basics Inc.
MY-K FORMULA 77 - Pharmaceutical - Pharmaceutical Basics Inc.
MY-K FORMULA 77D - Pharmaceutical - Pharmaceutical Basics Inc.
MY-LADY - Hosiery and underwear - Moyer Co. Inc., Walter W.
MY LADY - Optical products - Art-Craft Optical Co.
MY LADY - Wine - Duplin Wine Cellars Inc. - NBMD
MY LIL BAT - Toy baseball bat - Renzi Plastic Corp., A. J.
MY LI'L KITCHEN - Toy - Tomy Corp.
MY LIL SWING - Swing toy - Renzi Plastic Corp., A. J.
MY-LITE - Lamps - Mobilite-Spartus - OP
MY LITTLE MARINA - Infants' bath toy - Century Products Inc.
MY LITTLE ONE NURSERY - Play center for dolls - Today's Kids
MY LITTLE PONY - Footwear - Pony Sports & Leisure Inc. - FND
MY LITTLE PONY - Game, puzzles - Bradley Co., Milton
MY LITTLE PONY - Plaything, activity toys - Hasbro Inc.
MY LITTLE PONY - Toy dresser sets - A.R.C.
MY LITTLE PONY FLUTTER PONIES - Puzzles - Bradley Co., Milton
MY LITTLE PONY MERRY-GO-ROUND - Game, now out of production - Bradley Co., Milton
MY LITTLE SHOWER - Infants' bath toy - Century Products Inc.
MY LOVE - Sterling flatware - Wallace Silversmiths - GTR
MY LOVE BUG - Product description unknown - Stuart Inc. - PDI
MY LUVIN' HEART - Toy - Fun World Inc.
MY MARYLAND MY MARYLAND - Recording label, now out of production - Evans Records Group, Frank
MY MASTERPIECE - Woodwind-instrument reeds - French American Reeds Manufacturing - GMI
MY MELODY - Hooked rugs - Capel Inc.
MY MICHELLE - Apparel - Fritzi of California Manufacturing Corp.
MY NAILS - Nail- and body-care franchise - Nailcare Inc. - DFO
MY-NAME - Pens - Sakura of America
MY NAME - Personal printer - Duke Co., Ronald K. - OP
MY NAME - Recording label, now out of production - Pickwick International Inc. - GM
MY-NAME - Stamp sets - Consolidated Stamp Manufacturing Co. Inc. - OP
MY NAME - Stationery embosser - Art Seal & Embosser Co. - OP
MY OFFICE - Computer software - Datapak Software Inc.
MY OWN - Feminine-hygiene products - Schering Corp. - DRB
MY OWN MEALS - My Own Meals Inc.
MY PAD - Infants' changing and shopping-cart pads - Pansy Ellen Products Inc.
MY PADS - Woodwind pads - Pizzi, Enzo - MMR
MY PAL - Gloves - Knoxville Glove Co.
MY PET - Pet-care products - My Pet Grooming Center
MY PET BEAR - Stuffed toy - Mattel Inc.
MY PET BUNNY - Stuffed toy - Mattel Inc.
MY PET KITTEN - Stuffed toy - Mattel Inc.
MY PET MONSTER - Catch mitts, now out of production - Synergistics Research Corp.
MY PET MONSTER - Plush toy, now out of production - Those Characters From Cleveland Inc.
MY PET PUPPY - Stuffed toy - Mattel Inc.
MY PHONEBOOK - Computer software - Nine Ninetyfive Businessware
MY PRECIOUS PUFFS - Dolls - Matchbox Toys USA
MY-PREFERENCE - Paprika - Marmorek & Son, Herbert
MY PRETTY PURSE - Toy - Fisher-Price Toys
MY-PRIDE - Citrus products - Myakka Processors Inc. - CFP
MY PRINCESS BY GIOVANNI - Jewelry - Giovanni Jewelry Co. - GAZ
MY RO - Sealers, tapes, caulking, etc. - Myro Inc. - BSN
MY SECRET - Carpet - Evans-Black Carpet Mills
MY SECRET - Cologne - CTS Laboratories Inc. - DRB
MY SELECTION - Chocolates - Hooper's Confections Inc. - CB
MY SHADOW - Postcards - The Exclusive Co. - GDA
MY SIN - Fragrance, bath oil, dusting powder, soap, etc. - Charles of the Ritz Group Ltd. - DRB
MY SIN - Optical products - Zyloware Corp.
MY SKIN - Foundation garments - Warnaco Inc.
MY SOLE - Women's shoes - Famolare Inc. - FND
MY SON THE DOCTOR - Game, now out of production - CFC Games - GDA
MY STARS - Tea - Coffee & Tea Ltd. - TBG
MY STICKER ALBUM BOOK - Creative Teaching Press Inc. - THC
MY SWEET - Optical products - Hudson Optical Corp.
MY SWEET MERMAID - Doll - Tomy Corp.

An entry from *Brands and Their Companies, Vol. 1, A-O,* p. 923. Edited by Donna Wood. Copyright © 1990 by Gale Research Inc. Reprinted with permission.

Brands and Their Companies. **Company name listings**

W

Company address code designation:
□ = Out of business

W & F MANUFACTURING CO. INC., THE, Box 126, Buffalo, NY 14240 (716)874-5850

W & H MANUFACTURERS, Industrial Site, Box 266, Nebraska City, NE 68410 - *FI* (402)873-5202

W & P CO., 380 Swift Ave., Unit 3, South San Francisco, CA 94080 - *OP* (415)871-6698

W & W MEATS INC., 2394 Canal Rd., Cleveland, OH 44113 - *QFF* (216)621-7846

W FASHION IMPORT, Address unknown - *MW*

W-K IMPORTS INC., Address unknown - *GDA*

WA MAC INC., Box 128, Carlstadt, NJ 07072 - *NSGA* (201)438-7200

WABA CO., Box 1907, Beverly Hills, CA 90213 - *GDA* (714)261-7119

WACHTEL BISCUIT, 445 S. Franklin, Hempstead, NY 11550 (516)538-3900

WACHTEL MUSIC PRODUCTS, Address unknown - *MMR*

WACHTER, FREDERICK J., 915 Lois Ln., Glenview, IL 60025 - *JCK* (312)724-0214

WACOAL AMERICA INC., 40 Triangle Blvd., Carlstadt, NY 07072 (201)933-8400

WADDELL MANUFACTURING CO. [Div. of Baker McMillen Co.], Box 2996, Grand Rapids, MI 49501 - *BSN* (616)454-8328

WADE PHARMACAL CO., Address unknown - *DRB*

WADERS, RALPH, 24-30 41st St., Astoria, NY 11103 - *PDI* (718)726-2023

WADIWALKERS INC., 6065 N.W. 167th St., B-7, Miami, FL 33015 - *FND* (305)825-9556

WADSWORTH INC. [of International Thomson], 10 Davis Dr., Belmont, CA 94002 (415)595-2350

WAECHTERSBACH USA INC. [of Waechtersbacher Keramik], 8300 N.E. Underground, Kansas City, MO 64161 - *CGT* (816)455-3800

WAERTSILA CORP., Address unknown

WAFER MACHE INC., 16 Elmgate Rd., Marlton, NJ 08053

WAFFLE HOUSE INC., 5986 Financial Dr., Norcross, GA 30071 - *DFO* (404)447-4488

WAGGING TAIL LTD., 95 River St., Hoboken, NJ 07030 - *PSM* (201)792-5321

WAGGONER CANDY CO., Address unknown - *CB*

WAGMAN & CO., N., 200 Lexington Ave., Hackensack, NJ 07601 - *GB* (201)489-0466

WAGNER & SONS, JOHN, Box C-5013, Ivyland, PA 18974 (215)674-5000

WAGNER AWNING & MANUFACTURING CO., THE, 2658 Scranton Rd. at Barber Ave., Cleveland, OH 44113 - (216)861-5400

WAGNER BROS. FEED CORP., 399 Conklin St., Suite 310, Farmingdale, NY 11735 - *PD* (516)293-2450

WAGNER CO. INC., CURTIS, Box 55753, Houston, TX 77255 (713)862-8410

WAGNER CORP., N., Address unknown - *GDA*

WAGNER ELECTRIC CO., 100 Misty Ln., Parsippany, NJ 07054 (201)386-9300

WAGNER EXCELLO FOODS INC., 10507 Delta Pkwy., Schiller Park, IL 60176 (312)671-6110

WAGNER FARMS MAGIC POP POPCORN, 29808 Brant Rd., Colon, MI 49040 (616)432-3251

WAGNER GROUP INC., 19804 Nordhoff Pl., Chatsworth, CA 91311 - *MMR* (818)765-0866

WAGNER HEALTH FOOD PRODUCTS - See WAGNER EXCELLO FOODS INC.

WAGNER INC., WARREN, Drawer 280, Crystal City, TX 78839 - *TGR* (512)374-3423

WAGNER JUICE CO. [Div. of Everfresh Inc.], Box 789, Franklin Park, IL 60131 - (312)833-8440

WAGNER MILLS, Box 545, Schuyler, NE 68661 (402)352-2971

WAGNER PRODUCTS [Div. of E. R. Wagner Manufacturing Co.], 331 Riverview Dr., Hustisford, WI 53034 (414)349-3271

WAGNER PUBLISHING, ROGER, 1050 Pioneer Way, El Cajon, CA 92021 (619)442-0522

WAGNER SALES, BILL, Address unknown - *GDA*

WAGNER SPRAY TECH, 1770 Fernbrook Ln., Minneapolis, MN 55441 - *BSN* (612)553-7000

WAGNER VINEYARDS, Rte. 414, Lodi, NY 14860 - *WAV* (607)582-6450

WAH YET INC., 510 3rd St., Floor M, Box 23, San Francisco, CA 94107 - *HFB* (415)981-5148

WAHL CLIPPER CORP., 2900 N. Locust St., Box 578, Sterling, IL 61081 - *DRB* (815)625-6525

WAHL CO., AUSTIN, 53 W. Jackson Blvd., Chicago, IL 60604 - *JCK* (312)922-3331

WAHLFELD MANUFACTURING CO., 1100 S.W. Washington St., Peoria, IL 61602 - *BSN* (309)673-4421

WAHPETON CANVAS CO. INC., 2217 N. 9th St., Wahpeton, ND 58075 - *BSN* (701)642-8787

WAIT-CAHILL CO., 704 N. Monroe St., Decatur, IL 62522 - *DRB* (217)422-2334

WAKE-BROOK HOUSE, 2609 N.E. 29th Ct., Fort Lauderdale, FL 33306

WAKE UP OIL CO., Box 66430, Indianapolis, IN 46268 - *NPN* (317)872-5505

WAKEFERN FOOD CORP., 600 York St., Elizabeth, NJ 07207 - *TGR* (201)527-3300

WAKMANN WATCH CO. INC., 20 E. 46th St., New York, NY 10017 - *JCK* (212)661-0606

WAKUNAGA OF AMERICA CO. LTD. [Div. of Wakunaga Pharmaceutical Co. Ltd.], 23501 Madero, Mission Viejo, CA 92691 (714)855-2776

WAL-JAN SURGICAL PRODUCTS INC - See HOME-AID DISTRIBUTORS

WAL-MART STORES INC., 702 S.W. 8th St., Bentonville, AR 72716 (501)273-4000

WAL-RICH CORP., 97-36 43rd Ave., Corona, NY 11368 - *HA* (718)476-7888

WALBEAD INC., 21 Hall St., Brooklyn, NY 11205 - *NFM* (718)855-4640

WALBORG CORP., 136 Madison Ave., New York, NY 10016 - *AR* (212)689-4222

WALBRAND INTERNATIONAL LTD., Address unknown

WALBRO CORP., 6242 Garfield St., Cass City, MI 487261397 - *LT* (517)872-2131

WALBRO MANUFACTURING CO. - See WALLACE BROS. MANUFACTURING CO.

WALBUCK CRAYON CO., 210 Andover St., Wilmington, MA 01887 - *OP*

WALCH, PUBLISHER, J. WESTON, Box 658, Portland, ME 04104 (207)772-2846

WALCO-LINCK CORP., 1234 U.S. Hwy. 46, Clifton, NJ 07013 - *DRB* (201)471-1070

WALCO STAINLESS [Div. of Utica Cutlery Co.], 820 Noyes, Utica, NY 13502 - *JCK* (315)733-4663

WALCO TOY CO. INC., 21 Hall St., Brooklyn, NY 11205 - *PDI*

WALD DESIGNS [Div. of BDW Inc.], 6679-K Peachtree Industrial Blvd., Norcross, GA 30092 - *PSM* (800)543-9253

WALD SOUND INC., 11131 Dora St., Sun Valley, CA 91352 - *CE* (213)875-0480

WALDBAUM CO., MILTON G., 501 N. Main St., Wakefield, NE 68784 - *TGR* (402)287-2211

WALDBAUM INC., Hemlock St. & Boulevard Ave., Central Islip, NY 11722 - *TGR* (516)582-9300

WALDEN FARMS INC. - See WFI CORP.

WALDEN FOOTWEAR CORP., Address unknown - *FND*

WALDENSIAN BAKERIES INC., 1611 E. Dixon Blvd., Shelby, NC 28150 - *TGR* (704)487-7232

WALDES TRUARC INC. [Div. of SKF Industries], 29-01 Borden Ave., Box 1030, Long Island City, NY 111014478 (718)392-3100

WALDMAN CORP., Address unknown - *JCK*

WALDMAN'S MEATS INC., Box 629, New Castle, PA 16103 - *QFF* (412)658-7788

WALDOM ELECTRONICS INC., 4339 W. 69th St., Chicago, IL 60629 - *MMR* (312)585-1212

WALDOR PRODUCTS, 132 Mallory Ave., Jersey City, NJ 07304 - *MM* (201)332-8650

WALGREEN CO., 200 Wilmot Rd., Deerfield, IL 60015 (312)940-2500

WALK CORP., BENJAMIN, 100 Main St., Unit #6, Somersworth, NH 03878 - *FND* (603)692-4870

WALK-OVER SHOES [Div. of Geo. E. Keith Co.], 31 Perkins St., Bridgewater, MA 02324 - *MW* (617)697-6104

WALKER & CO., Address unknown - *GM*

WALKER & SON, W. H., R.D.1 Box 12, Rte. 44-55, Clintondale, NY 12515 - *TGR* (914)883-5546

WALKER & SONS APIARIES, Address unknown - *TGR*

WALKER & ZANGER INC., 179 Summerfield St., Scarsdale, NY 10583 (914)472-5666

WALKER CO., THE, Address unknown - *DRB*

TM 138   OFFICIAL GAZETTE   APRIL 3, 1990

CLASS 37—(Continued).

SN 73-806,401. MR. FIXIT AUTOMOTIVE & TIRE CEN-
TERS INC., DELRAY BEACH, FL. FILED 6-26-1989.

NO CLAIM IS MADE TO THE EXCLUSIVE RIGHT TO
USE "FIXIT", APART FROM THE MARK AS SHOWN.
THE MARK CONSISTS OF THE LETTERS "X" IN
STYLIZED FORM AND A REPRESENTATION OF
WRENCHES.
FOR MAINTENANCE AND REPAIR OF AUTOMO-
BILES; TIRE ROTATING AND BALANCING SERVICES;
AND AUTOMOBILE LUBRICATION SERVICES (U.S. CL.
103).
FIRST USE 1-0-1989; IN COMMERCE 1-0-1989.

—————

SN 73-808,876. ANTON/BAUER, INC., SHELTON, CT.
FILED 6-26-1989.

THE QUALITY STANDARD
OF THE VIDEO INDUSTRY

FOR MANUFACTURE AND SERVICING OF PROD-
UCTS FOR THE PROFESSIONAL VIDEO INDUSTRY
(U.S. CLS. 100, 101 AND 103).
FIRST USE 12-0-1982; IN COMMERCE 12-0-1982.

CLASS 37—(Continued).

SN 73-814,805. TRANSCONTINENTAL PROPERTIES, INC.,
SCOTTSDALE, AZ. FILED 7-24-1989.

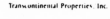

NO CLAIM IS MADE TO THE EXCLUSIVE RIGHT TO
USE "TRANSCONTINENTAL PROPERTIES, INC.",
APART FROM THE MARK AS SHOWN.
THE LINING SHOWN IN THE DRAWING IS A FEA-
TURE OF THE MARK AND NOT INTENDED TO INDI-
CATE COLOR.
FOR REAL ESTATE LAND DEVELOPMENT SERV-
ICES (U.S. CL. 103).
FIRST USE 1-1-1989; IN COMMERCE 1-1-1989.

—————

SN 73-815,142. PERMA-BUILT BY BRIGHT, INC., TULSA,
OK. FILED 7-27-1989.

FOR FOUNDATION CONSTRUCTION, MAINTE-
NANCE, AND REPAIR SERVICES (U.S. CL. 103).
FIRST USE 5-14-1989; IN COMMERCE 5-14-1989.

—————

SN 73-830,568. BENTON FOUNDRY, INC., BENTON, PA.
FILED 10-10-1989.

FOR FOUNDRY SERVICES (U.S. CL. 103).
FIRST USE 1-1-1986; IN COMMERCE 1-1-1986.

Official Gazette. **Trademark registrations**

1,589,680. **CITRIX.** HUANG, JERRY T., DBA DENTAMER-ICA FOR ROYAL INDUSTRIES, (U.S. CL. 44). SN 73-813,185. PUB. 1-9-1990. FILED 7-17-1989.

1,589,681. **PHONE SENSE.** PHONE SENSE LTD., (U.S. CL. 6). SN 73-813,290. PUB. 1-9-1990. FILED 7-18-1989.

1,589,682. **DIVIDEND.** CIBA-GEIGY CORPORATION, (U.S. CL. 6). SN 73-814,751. PUB. 1-9-1990. FILED 7-25-1989.

1,589,683. **MISCELLANEOUS DESIGN.** MEAD JOHNSON & COMPANY, (U.S. CL. 18). SN 73-814,869. PUB. 1-9-1990. FILED 7-24-1989.

1,589,684. **TECHNESCAN.** MALLINCKRODT, INC., (U.S. CLS. 18 AND 38). SN 73-815,124. PUB. 1-9-1990. FILED 7-27-1989.

1,589,685. **ANASED.** VET-A-MIX, INC., (U.S. CL. 18). SN 73-815,445. PUB. 1-9-1990. FILED 7-28-1989.

1,589,686. **FIRST MILK.** FEED SPECIALTIES CO., INC., (U.S. CL. 18). SN 73-815,603. PUB. 1-9-1990. FILED 7-31-1989.

1,589,687. **RACE CAPS.** HANSEN & FRANK, (U.S. CL. 18). SN 73-816,412. PUB. 1-9-1990. FILED 8-1-1989.

1,589,688. **3M (STYLIZED).** MINNESOTA MINING AND MANUFACTURING COMPANY, AKA 3M, (U.S. CLS. 18 AND 37). SN 73-817,909. PUB. 1-9-1990. FILED 8-8-1989.

1,589,689. **EFODINE.** ALTANA, INC., (U.S. CL. 18). SN 73-818,016. PUB. 1-9-1990. FILED 8-9-1989.

1,589,690. **VANTAGE.** ELI LILLY AND COMPANY, (U.S. CL. 18). SN 73-818,192. PUB. 1-9-1990. FILED 8-9-1989.

1,589,691. **ENABLE.** PFIZER INC., (U.S. CL. 18). SN 73-818,321. PUB. 1-9-1990. FILED 8-10-1989.

1,589,692. **CITALOR.** PFIZER INC., (U.S. CL. 18). SN 73-818,322. PUB. 1-9-1990. FILED 8-10-1989.

1,589,693. **COGMINE.** FOREST LABORATORIES, INC., (U.S. CL. 18). SN 73-818,341. PUB. 1-9-1990. FILED 8-10-1989.

1,589,694. **LIFE BALANCE AND DESIGN.** LIFESCIENCE TECHNOLOGIES, INC., (U.S. CLS. 18 AND 46). SN 73-818,386. PUB. 1-9-1990. FILED 8-10-1989.

1,589,695. **PRIME.** ROLF C. HAGEN (USA) CORP., (U.S. CL. 18). SN 73-818,622. PUB. 1-9-1990. FILED 8-11-1989.

1,589,696. **MINO-TABS.** AMERICAN CYANAMID COMPANY, (U.S. CL. 18). SN 73-818,768. PUB. 1-9-1990. FILED 8-9-1989.

1,589,697. **NEPHRO-VITE.** R & D LABORATORIES INC., (U.S. CL. 18). SN 73-819,572. PUB. 1-9-1990. FILED 8-16-1989.

1,589,698. **DIVARIA.** ABBOTT LABORATORIES, (U.S. CL. 6). SN 73-819,655. PUB. 1-9-1990. FILED 8-16-1989.

1,589,699. **TIME IS MUSCLE.** GENENTECH, INC., (U.S. CL. 18). SN 73-819,840. PUB. 1-9-1990. FILED 8-17-1989.

1,589,700. **COLON-EZE.** GREAT EARTH DISTRIBUTION, INC., (U.S. CL. 18). SN 73-820,210. PUB. 1-9-1990. FILED 8-21-1989.

1,589,701. **MIKRO-CHLOR.** ECOLAB INC., (U.S. CL. 6). SN 73-820,579. PUB. 1-9-1990. FILED 8-21-1989.

1,589,702. **BOUQUET AIRE.** WILLERT HOME PRODUCTS, INC., (U.S. CL. 6). SN 73-822,676. PUB. 1-9-1990. FILED 8-31-1989.

1,589,703. **CLEARASIL CLEARSTICK.** RICHARDSON-VICKS INC., (U.S. CL. 18). SN 73-825,334. PUB. 1-9-1990. FILED 9-14-1989.

CLASS 6—METAL GOODS

1,589,704. **Z AND DESIGN.** FRIEDRICH WILHELM FURST VON HOHENZOLLERN, DBA FURSTLICH HOHEN-ZOLLERNSCHE HUTTENVERWALTUNG LAU-CHERTHAL, MULTIPLE CLASS, (INT. CLS. 6 AND 7), (U.S. CLS. 13, 14 AND 23). SN 73-591,531. PUB. 1-9-1990. FILED 4-3-1986.

1,589,705. **VHP HUNGARIAN SYSTEM AND DESIGN.** VESZPREMI SZENBANYAK, MULTIPLE CLASS, (INT. CLS. 6 AND 7), (U.S. CLS. 13 AND 23). SN 73-701,706. PUB. 1-9-1990. FILED S.R. 12-18-1987; AM. P.R. 3-14-1988.

1,589,706. **SOVEREIGN.** MAJCO BUILDING SPECIAL-TIES, L.P., (U.S. CL. 25). SN 73-775,590. PUB. 1-9-1990. FILED 1-23-1989.

1,589,707. **LIFETIME.** JULIUS BLUM G.M.B.H., MULTIPLE CLASS, (INT. CLS. 6 AND 20), (U.S. CL. 13). SN 73-786,734. PUB. 1-9-1990. FILED 3-14-1989.

1,589,708. **TABFOIL.** PHOENIX CLOSURES, INC., (U.S. CLS. 14 AND 50). SN 73-810,249. PUB. 1-9-1990. FILED 7-3-1989.

1,589,709. **YFS.** FANG SHENG SCREW CO., LTD., (U.S. CL. 13). SN 73-812,382. PUB. 1-9-1990. FILED 7-14-1989.

1,589,710. **RHINO AND DESIGN.** RHINO, INC., (U.S. CLS. 2 AND 14). SN 73-820,973. PUB. 1-9-1990. FILED 8-22-1989.

1,589,711. **MB 1320 ADVANTAGE ROLLAWAY.** JACOBS MANUFACTURING COMPANY, THE, (U.S. CL. 2). SN 73-821,523. PUB. 1-9-1990. FILED 8-25-1989.

1,589,712. **PAC-CLAD.** PETERSEN ALUMINUM CORPO-RATION, (U.S. CLS. 6 AND 14). SN 73-822,735. PUB. 1-9-1990. FILED 8-31-1989.

CLASS 7—MACHINERY

1,589,704 (*See Class 6 for this trademark*).

1,589,705 (*See Class 6 for this trademark*).

1,589,713. **AQUA POWER MARINE PRODUCTS.** AQUA POWER CORPORATION, (U.S. CL. 23). SN 73-756,416. PUB. 1-9-1990. FILED 10-7-1988.

1,589,714. **SAW-SAFE.** EISTRAT, THOMAS, DBA SAW-SAFE, (U.S. CL. 23). SN 73-758,819. PUB. 1-9-1990. FILED 12-30-1988.

1,589,715. **POWERSPAN.** SYSTEMS, INC., (U.S. CLS. 12 AND 23). SN 73-763,231. PUB. 1-9-1990. FILED 11-14-1988.

1,589,716. **ULTRAMAG (STYLIZED).** NOMA INC., (U.S. CLS. 19 AND 21). SN 73-777,159. PUB. 1-9-1990. FILED 2-9-1989.

1,589,717. **DOUBLE CUT.** C.F.C. DISTRIBUTORS, INC., (U.S. CL. 23). SN 73-778,242. PUB. 1-9-1990. FILED 2-2-1989.

1,589,718. **FT8.** TURBO POWER AND MARINE SYSTEMS, INC., (U.S. CL. 23). SN 73-781,872. PUB. 1-9-1990. FILED 2-21-1989.

1,589,719. **ISOA.** TOMOE VALVE CO., LTD., (U.S. CL. 23). SN 73-784,477. PUB. 1-9-1990. FILED 3-3-1989.

1,589,720. **MILCLAW.** MILLS MACHINE COMPANY, (U.S. CL. 23). SN 73-784,592. PUB. 1-9-1990. FILED 3-3-1989.

1,589,721. **SENSOFLEX (BLOCK FORM).** BARRY WRIGHT CORPORATION, (U.S. CL. 23). SN 73-785,486. PUB. 1-9-1990. FILED 3-9-1989.

1,589,722. **CERAMITRON.** F. C. HOLDINGS, INC., (U.S. CL. 23). SN 73-793,954. PUB. 1-9-1990. FILED 4-17-1989.

1,589,723. **MISCELLANEOUS DESIGN.** CLOUD CORPORA-TION, MULTIPLE CLASS, (INT. CLS. 7 AND 35), (U.S. CLS. 23, 101 AND 105). SN 73-795,322. PUB. 1-9-1990. FILED 4-24-1989.

1,589,724. **RADIARC.** WALDRUM SPECIALTIES, INC., (U.S. CL. 23). SN 73-797,102. PUB. 1-9-1990. FILED 5-1-1989.

1,589,725. **BILTUP.** CRANE MANUFACTURING & SERV-ICE CORPORATION, (U.S. CL. 23). SN 73-800,720. PUB. 1-9-1990. FILED 5-16-1989.

1,589,726. **JET-PAC (STYLIZED).** SCHAFFNER MANUFAC-TURING COMPANY, INC., (U.S. CL. 23). SN 73-801,134. PUB. 1-9-1990. FILED 5-19-1989.

1,589,727. **HOFFMAN.** ITT CORPORATION, (U.S. CLS. 13 AND 23). SN 73-804,195. PUB. 1-9-1990. FILED 6-2-1989.

1,589,728. **SUPER SHREDDER.** FRANKLIN MILLER INC., (U.S. CL. 23). SN 73-804,226. PUB. 1-9-1990. FILED 6-5-1989.

1,589,729. **DURAKING.** DANA CORPORATION, (U.S. CLS. 23 AND 35). SN 73-810,346. PUB. 1-9-1990. FILED 7-3-1989.

1,589,730. **MISCELLANEOUS DESIGN.** FARMHAND, INC., (U.S. CL. 23). SN 73-810,428. PUB. 1-9-1990. FILED 7-3-1989.

The Trade Register. **Trademarks directory, international classes section**

INTERNATIONAL CLASS 9 – 775

STELCO - US 21.. 9-5-78...1,101,282
STELLA - US 27... 4-14-64...768,177
STELLA - US 21,26... 8-18-87...1,452,967
STELLA - US 38 .. 5-17 88...1,488,203
STELLA AND DESIGN - US 38... 8-22-89...1,552,580
STELLAR - US 26 7-12-83 1,245,122
STELLAR - US 21,26... 1-31-84.. 1,265,617
STELLAR - US 38.. 9-27-88 ..1,505,650
STELLAR AND DESIGN - US 21... 7-16-63.. 752,849
STELLARSONIC - US 21 .. 7-12-83... 1,245,120
STELLAR SYSTEMS - US 21,26 6-25-85...1,343,955
STELLAR SYSTEMS AND DESIGN - US 21,26... 6-25-85 ..1,343,954
STELLAR TOWER BELLS - US 36... 12-2-75...1,026,092
STELLIX - US 38... 5-10-88 ..1,487,459
STELPLAN - US 38... 11-19-85...1,370,971
STEMCO - US 26... 3-23-54...587,202
STEMCO AND DESIGN - US 21.. 11-23-54...598,430
STEMCO AND DESIGN - US 23,26... 12-2-86 ..1,418,935
STEMCO-ENGLER - US 26... 5-27-86...1,394,705
STEMCO-MONROE - US 23,26... 12-16-86...1,420,805
STEMI - US 26... 2-10-87...1,428,217
S-TEMP - US 26... 2-2-82...1,188,519
STEN - US 26,38.. 3-15-83...1,230,895
STENDHAL - US 26... 7-8-86...1,400,189
STENED - US 21,36,38... 8-22-89...1,552,705
STENO-CAT - US 26... 7-6-82...1,200,302
STENOCORD - US 21,26,36... 1-2-79...1,110,425
STENODATA - US 26... 1-8-80...1,128,894
STENOMASK - US 21... 12-7-54...598,990
STENOPROMPTER - US 21... 1-7-58...656,744
STENORAM - US 26... 3-12-85...1,324,129
STENORETTE - US 21... 2-21-56...621,737
STENORETTE - US 26... 1-3-78...1,080,863
STENORETTE - US 21... 1-3-78...1,080,863
STENTOFON - US 21... 12-3-68...861,319
"STEP BY STEP-GROWING UP HEALTHY" - US 21... 12-5-89...1,569,365
STEP IVWARD - US 38... 9-5-89...1,554,515
STEP PAK AND DESIGN - US 26... 9-23-86...1,410,271
STEPPENWOLF - US 21,36... 3-29-88...1,482,170
STEPPER - US 26... 11-29-83...1,259,243
STEP-PETTE - US 26... 6-4-85...1,338,979
STEPPING OUT - US 38... 5-3-88...1,486,836
STEPPINGSTONES - US 36... 9-23-86...1,410,252
STEPPIN' OUT - US 21... 9-21-82...1,209,591
STEPS - US 38... 4-5-88...1,483,195
STEP-SAVER - US 38... 12-17-85...1,375,643
STEP SAVER - US 21... 6-17-86...1,397,502
STEP-SAVER ACCOUNTING MANAGEMENT SYSTEM - US 38,101... 9-29-87...1,459,005
STEP-SAVER AND DESIGN - US 38 .. 11-25-86...1,418,224
STEP-SAVER DATA SYSTEMS - US 38,100... 7-21-87 ..1,448,241
STEP-SAVER LEGAL SYSTEMS - US 38,100... 8-25-87...1,454,003
STEP-SAVER MEDICAL PRACTICE MANAGEMENT SYSTEM - US 38 9-1-87...1,454,939
STEP-SAVER MPMS - US 38.. 8-26-86...1,406,613
STEPSCAN - US 21 7-18-78...1,096,557
STEP START - US 26.. 7-21-87...1,449,087
STEP START - US 26 11-14-89 1,565,572
STEPSTONE - US 38... 4-4-89 1,532,780
STEP UP USED CARS - US 21,36,37,38 .. 10-20-87 ..1,461,728
STEP 1 - US 38 .. 7-16-85...1,348,975
STEREMOTE - US 21,26... 6-7-83...1,240,929
STEREO BUTLER - US 21,26.. 9-29-87.. 1,459,079
STEREO COMPUTER - US 21,36... 4-8-86...1,389,516
STEREO/DIMENSIONAL ARRAY - US 21... 10-2-84 ..1,298,466
STEREO EVERYWHERE - US 21... 9-9-86...1,408,266
STEREO-FIDELITY AND DESIGN - US 36... 9-3-63 756,071
STEREOHEDRON - US 21... 4-17-79...1,116,566
STEREOLITH - US 21,36 .. 12-8-87...1,468,099
STEREOMASTER AND DESIGN - US 26... 10-23-84...1,301,373
STEREO MATE - US 21... 8-16-83 ..1,248,212
STEREO-MATE - US 36... 8-16-83...1,248,213
STEREO-MATIC - US 26... 10-26-54...597,339
STEREO-MATIC - US 21... 10-2-56...635,109
STEREO MICRO - US 36... 5-27-86...1,395,383
STEREOMIXER - US 21,36... 5-23-89...1,541,065
STEREOPHONIZER - US 21... 7-28-81...1,162,545
STEREO.PLEXER - US 21... 2-26-85...1,321,918
STEREOPTIC - US 26... 7-16-68...852,700
STEREOPYCNOMETER - US 26 3-22-83...1,231,737
STEREORAMA - US 26... 5-10-55 605,782
STEREOSCAN - US 21... 1-11-66...801,731
STEREOSCAN - US 26... 5-28-68 ..849,781
STEREOSCHUTTLE AND DESIGN - US 21... 3-18-86 ..1,386,587
STEREO SPACE - US 21... 10-4-88...1,506,970
STEREO SPORTS - US 21,36... 8-14-84 ..1,289,887
STEREO TARGETING - US 21... 9-15-87...1,457,280
STEREO TEK - US 21,26,38.. 5-31-88...1,489,945
STEREOTEK - US 21,26,38... 5-31-88...1,489,946
STEREO THEATRE - US 21... 5-25-65...789,924
STEREOTRON - US 21... 5-22-84...1,278,796
STERILIGHT - US 26,34... 7-18-89...1,548,019
STERI LINE - US 26... 11-22-55...615,528
STERI-LOOP - US 26... 7-23-85 ..1,350,486
STERIREGISTER - US 21... 6-25-68 ..851,364
STERISENS - US 23,26... 1-5-88 ..1,471,196
STERISYSTEMS - US 21... 5-27-69 869,998
STERITAB - US 26... 10-15-85...1,365,286
STERITEMP - US 44... 12-23-80 ..1,143,958
STERITEST - US 26... 7-23-68 853,189
STERIVISION - US 21... 11-22-66 819,040
STERLIUN - US 26... 6-14-83...1,241,887
STERLING - US 21,23,38,103 .. 9-28-82...1,210,255
STERLING - US 21... 11-22-83...1,258,394
STERLING - US 21,23,34... 11-19-85 ..1,370,950
STERLING - US 26,52... 11-14-89...1,565,677
STERLING•AUTOTEST AND DESIGN - US 38... 11-14-89...1,565,691
STERLING OPTICAL AN IPCO COMPANY AND DESIGN - US 26... 5-25-82...1,196,151
STERLING OPTICAL, DES. - US 26... 7-5-77...1,069,305
STERLING SOFTWARE SS AND DESIGN - US 38.. 10-6-87 ..1,459,940
STERN-GUARD - US 21... 10-18-88...1,509,040
STETHOCLINIC - US 36... 9-27-60...704,969
STETOMIKE - US 21... 5-31-83...1,240,138
STETSON - US 26... 10-18-83...1,254,420
STEVECO - US 21... 10-11-66...816,541
STEVECO - US 21... 2-1-77...1,057,449
STEVEDORE - US 38... 11-8-88...1,511,593
STEVEN - US 21... 11-1-88...1,510,742
STEVENS - US 21,26... 12-22-81...1,182,797
STEVENS-ARNOLD - US 21... 6-28-83...1,243,450
STEVENS FOTO SIZING SYSTEM AND DESIGN - US 26... 5-31-88...1,489,983
STEVENS TELEMARK - US 26... 9-11-62...737,516
STEVE STRALEY'S CLIRMA LIBRARY - US 38... 10-24-89...1,561,938
STEVE STRALEY'S TOOLKIT - US 38... 8-29-89...1,553,591
STEWARD - US 21,36... 6-19-79...1,120,413
STEWART FILMSCREEN AND DESIGN - US 26... 8-26-69...875,607
STEWART SW WARNER AND DESIGN - US 26... 1-12-60...691,251
STEWART-WARNER - US 26.. 4-14-59...676,953
STEWY - US 26... 2-10-76...1,032,881
ST-FIN - US 38... 9-26-89...1,557,786
STI - US 26... 10-18-83...1,254,385
STI - US 38... 5-14-85...1,335,228
STI AND DESIGN - US 26.. 10-4-77...1,074,470
STI AND DESIGN - US 21... 9-22-81 ..1,169,941
STIC KEYS - US 21... 5-6-86...1,392,221
STICKLER - US 26... 2-24-87...1,430,108
STICKS & BRICKS - US 38 .. 1-31-89 ..1,522,454
STICK-UP - US 21,23... 6-11-85.. 1,340,368
STICKY BUSINESS - US 38... 6-6-89...1,542,366
STI-CO - US 21.. 11-19-85...1,371,139
STIEBEL ELTRON - US 21,26,34 1-11-83.. 1,223,185
STIHL - US 23,26,39... 7-5-83 1,244,156
STIK-A-SWITCH - US 21... 9-23-86...1,410,275
STILAN - US 21... 5-13-75...1,010,344
STILLPILE - US 21,26,38... 8-15-89...1,551,707
STILLWATER DESIGNS - US 21 12-8-87...1,468,124
STIMPMETER - US 26... 7-4-89 1,546,904
STIMU-LENS - US 26... 3-28-89 1,531,720
STIMULOR - US 13,23,26,46... 7-30-85...1,351,346
STINES AND DESIGN - US 1,2,3,4,5,6,10,12, – 13,15,16,19,21,23,25,32,35,50,51,52... 3-27-84...1,271,369
THE STING - US 34... 10-2-84 1,298,644
STING - US 26... 7-21-87...1,448,303
THE STING AND DESIGN - US 34... 3-6-79...1,114,428
THE STINGER - US 23,26... 7-23-85...1,350,466
STINGER - US 21,36... 10-17-89 ..1,560,648
STINGER AND DESIGN - US 21... 11-9-76...1,052,325
STINGER AND DESIGN - US 21... 3-26-85...1,326,653
STING PRINT - US 11,26... 12-26-89...1,573,020
STING RAY - US 21... 11-9-65 ..798,494
STINGRAY - US 26... 10-8-85...1,364,299
STING-RAY AND DESIGN - US 26 .. 8-27-68...855,541
STIRELLA - US 26... 6-28-88...1,493,938
STIRLING POWER SYSTEMS AND DESIGN - US 19, 21... 12-22-81...1,182,749
STIR PAK - US 26... 9-16-75...1,019,887
STITCHER AND DESIGN - US 26... 4-10-84...1,273,379
STITCHES - US 38... 1-17-89...1,520,697
STITCH-FINDER - US 26... 2-12-85...1,320,129
STIWA AND DESIGN - US 23,26,32,100,101,103 .. 6-30-87...1,444,851
STL - US 23,26... 1-5-82...1,184,530
STM - US 26... 5-6-75...1,009,879
STM - US 21,26... 10-8-85...1,364,236
ST. MARYS AND DESIGN - US 21... 4-30-63...748,703
ST. MICHAEL - US 2,5,6,13,14,15,21,22,23, 26,27,28,29,32,37,38,44,51... 10-27-87...1,462,468
STMTUR - US 38... 4-23-85...1,331,799
STN COMMUNICATOR - US 38 .. 9-20-88...1,504,647
STN EXPRESS - US 38... 2-14-89...1,524,302
STN EXPRESS AND DESIGN - US 38... 2-14-89...1,524,301
STOCKO - US 13,21,23,25,38,40 12-3-85...1,373,399
STOCKPAK - US 38,102... 9-4-84 ..1,292,664
STOCKPLOT - US 38... 9-11-84...1,293,973
STOCKPRO - US 38... 5-27-86 1,394,721
STOCKRAY - US 26... 1-19-60 691,652
STOCKTRAC - US 38. 8-23-88 1,501,053
STOCKWATCH! - US 38... 8-4-87...1,450,449
STOMACHER - US 26... 9-2-75...1,019,260
STONE - US 21,36... 8-29-89...1,553,534
STONEHENGE - US 36... 2-11-86 1,382,153
STONE ISLAND AND DESIGN - US 3,8,22,26,27, 28,39,41,51,52... 7-18-89...1,547,865
STONE MOUNTAIN - US 3,8,26... 11-6-84...1,303,487
STONE PHONES - US 21... 11-14-89...1,565,655
STONER - US 21... 9-12-78...1,102,009
STONEWALL - US 26... 3-15-88...1,480,677
STOODEX - US 14... 4-12-77...1,063,212
STOODY - US 14,21,23,34,35... 11-1-83...1,255,801
STOP - US 21,26,34... 1-12-88...1,472,016
STOP GO AND DESIGN - US 21... 9-25-56...634,772
STOPINC - US 12,13,23,26... 5-3-88...1,486,685
STOPLOCK AND DESIGN - US 21.. 12-17-85...1,375,596
STOPMASTER - US 26... 11-3-81...1,175,986
STOP MESSING AROUND! - US 26... 8-16-88...1,500,373
STOPMETER - US 26... 3-16-54...587,097
STOP-ON-TOP - US 26... 7-11-89...1,547,200
STOPPER - US 21... 10-17-89...1,560,550
STOPPER LOC - US 26... 6-25-85...1,343,965
STOPWATCH BINGO AND DESIGN - US 21... 2-11-86...1,382,103
STOR-A-CORD - US 21... 4-19-83...1,235,513
STOR-A-CORD JR. - US 21... 10-2-84...1,298,464
STORAGE DIMENSIONS - US 26,38... 10-24-89...1,561,941
STORAGEMASTER - US 26... 2-12-85...1,319,118
STORAGEMASTER - US 26... 2-19-85...1,320,464
STORAGE SOLUTIONS - US 38... 8-22-89...1,552,622
STORAGETEK - US 26,38... 8-26-86...1,406,502
STORECASTING - US 21... 1-21-47...426,987
STOREDATA - US 26... 9-1-87...1,455,069
STORE FRONT RETAILING - US 38... 10-4-88...1,507,602
STOREHOUSE - US 38... 5-27-86.. 1,394,752
STOREKEEPER AND DESIGN - US 26,38... 4-18-89...1,535,047
THE STORE MANAGER - US 38... 3-15-83...1,230,879
STORENET/2 - US 38... 3-28-89...1,531,797
STORETALK - US 21,50... 10-11-88...1,507,936
STOREX - US 3,36... 11-17-87...1,465,206
STORK AND DESIGN - US 10,13,19,21,23,34,35,37.. 5-19-81...1,154,324
STORK RECORDS, INC. AND DESIGN - US 38,107... 8-23-83...1,248,855
STORM AND DESIGN - US 21... 12-2-86...1,419,019
STORM CHOKE - US 13... 4-12-60...695,910
STORMER - US 26... 9-15-81...1,169,041
STORM KING - US 9... 7-14-59...681,665
STORMOSCOPE - US 26... 12-31-63...762,297
STORM QUEEN - US 26... 11-1-88...1,510,793
STORMSCOPE - US 21,26... 5-8-79...1,117,583
STORM SENTRY AND DES. - US 21... 2-15-77 ..1,059,057
STORM TRAPPER - US 21... 7-16-85...1,349,041
STORMY SEAS - US 26,39... 6-10-86 ..1,396,611
STORMY SEAS FLOTATION FOR PROFESSIONALS AND DESIGN - US 26,39... 2-4-86...1,381,150
STORNO - US 21... 11-29-88...1,514,460
STORNOPHONE - US 21... 11-22-88...1,513,465
STOR 'N' STYLE - US 3,26... 7-22-86...1,402,023
STORSELECTOR SYSTEMS AND DESIGN - US 26... 11-10-87...1,464,411
STORTRAK AND DESIGN - US 38... 7-10-84...1,285,103
STORTZ AND DESIGN - US 26... 8-23-66...813,416
STORYBOARDER - US 38... 8-20-85...1,355,167
STORYBOOK HOUSE AND DESIGN - US 21,36,38 .. 9-19-89...1,556,577
STORYBOOKS BROUGHT TO LIFE - US 21 .. 5-20-86...1,393,890
STORY CASTLE - US 23... 10-11-77...1,074,899
STORYDISK AND DESIGN - US 38... 6-19-84...1,282,232
STORYLAND - US 21,36,38... 6-21-88...1,492,980
STORYLINE - US 38.. 11-13-84...1,304,794
STORY MAKER - US 38... 4-16-85...1,330,719
STORYTELLER - US 36,38... 8-25-81...1,166,227
STORYTELLING CIRCLE - US 21,36,38... 3-19-85...1,325,565
STORYTIME CLASSICS AND DESIGN - US 21... 4-1-86...1,388,122
STORY TREE - US 38... 5-7-85...1,334,083
STORZ AND DESIGN - US 26,36,44... 6-2-81...1,156,220
STORZ URBAN - US 21,26... 3-15-88...1,480,667
STOW - US 15,19,21,23... 1-3-84...1,262,797
STOW A VAC - US 23,26... 12-26-89...1,573,095
STOWAWAY - US 21... 7-17-79...1,122,256
STOWAWAY - US 21... 1-14-86...1,377,978
STOWE AND DESIGN - US 21,26... 9-26-89...1,557,699
STPM - US 26... 12-6-88...1,515,170

The Trade Register of the United States. 32nd ed., 1990, p. 775. Reprinted with permission.

The Compu-Mark Directory of U.S. Trademarks.

INTERNATIONAL CLASS 1

63 / PANOSCREEN

66 NO 22		R823552	**PANOSCREEN**·2·CHAS. PFIZER & CO., INC.
79 NO 20	142	R1130824	**PANSORBIN**·CALBIOCHEM-BEHRING CORP.
81 OC 13	·188	R1184325	**PANTALAST**·PANTASOTE INC.
58 MY 14		R853426	**THE PANTASOTE COMPANY**·2·PANTASOTE COM
53 MY 12	·311	RR578532	**PANTHER CREEK**·D2·AMERICAN COLLOID COMPA
69 AU 26		R880269	**PANTHER CREEK**·2·AMERICAN COLLOID COMPAN
83 MR 01	· 23	R1239044	**PANTRAK**·AMERICAN HOECHST CORPORATION
85 JA 07	PEN	SN516594	**SHEER SAVERS THE SPRAY THAT MAKES YOUR PANTYHOSE LAST LONGER.**·D·SHEER-SAVERS MANUFACTURING CANADA LTD.
66 JN 28		R814779	**PANYLEZE**·8·PANYL CORPORATION
84 MR 20	308	R1281138	**DAKO PAP KIT**·DAKOPATTS A/S
85 AU 21	PEN	SN554597	**KEY PAPER**·ORGENICS, LTD.
65 AP 20		RR732011	**INTERNATIONAL PAPER**·2·INTERNATIONAL PAPE
73 OC 23	239	R971637	**LIQUID PAPER**·D8·LIQUID PAPER CORPORATION
83 JA 11	·179	R1233190	**ALTERPRINT PAPER (BLOCK FORM)**·FAR WEST/MICROGRAPHIX, INC.
84 JL 24	·538	R1298284	**PAL PAPER PAL CHEMICAL CORPORATION**·D·PAL CHEMICAL CORPORATION
83 MR 22	507	R1241732	**PAPER QUICK**·CARPENTER PAPER COMPANY
73 JL 03	12	R966451	**'THE PAPER RABBIT'**·2·ORGANON INC
85 JA 15	405	R1326611	**PAPER-TEK**·DEARBORN CHEMICAL COMPANY
84 AP 24	·478	R1300029	**PAPERCHEM**·BETZ PAPERCHEM, INC.
		RR319689	**PAPERINE**·A.M. MEINCKE & SON, INC.
67 OC 24		R841868	**WORLD HEADQUARTERS FOR PAPERS AND CHEMICALS FOR THE NEEDLE TRADES**·D2·PRECISION PAPERS, INC.
72 NO 21	·230	R947757 S	**PAPERSCENT**·8·GIVAUDAN CORPORATION
58 JA 21		RR660264	**PAPI**·2·CARWIN COMPANY
69 NO 11		R885024	**PAPS**·2·AZOPLATE CORPORATION
83 AP 12	·168	R1244037	**NAPS/PAPS**·AMERICAN HOECHST CORPORATION
68 DE 10		R865145	**PAPYEX**·8·SOCIETE LE CARBONE LORRAINE
69 OC 14		R883136	**CYCLO-PAQUE**·8·DESERT MINERALS, INC.
72 MY 16		R939384	**PERMA-PAQUE**·2·ALFRED MOSSNER COMPANY
76 JA 06	·200	R1036505	**FICOLL-PAQUE**·2·PHARMACIA FINE CHEMICALS, IN
83 AU 09	·178	R1255675	**LYMPHO-PAQUE**·NYEGAARD & CO., A/S
69 AU 26		R892625	**PAR**·2·R. T. VANDERBILT COMPANY INC.
77 JL 26	·176	R1075302	**CHRONO-PAR**·8·CHRONO-LOG CORPORATION
81 FE 03	11	R1152031	**PAR**·D·ARMAK COMPANY
83 JA 11	·178	R1233182	**LIQUA PAR**·MALLINCKRODT, INC.
59 JN 23		RR684618	**PAR-EX**·2·SWIFT & COMPANY
59 JA 06		R675817	**PAR-O-LENE**·2·S. C. MCADAMS
65 MR 16		RR797411	**PAR-O-LENE**·2·PAR-O-LENE CHEMICAL CORPORATIO
76 MR 02	· 8	R1039966	**PAR/PAK**·2·BIO DATA CORPORATION
84 MY 22	·539	R1307584	**PARA**·STRECK LABORATORIES, INC.
48 SE 28	·840	RR511266	**PARA-FLUX**·2·C.P. HALL COMPANY
85 JL 16	28	R1361260	**PARA LASER**·STRECK LABORATORIES, INC.
81 MY 05	17	SN212665	**PARA-PAK**·MERIDIAN DIAGNOSTICS, INC.
48 FE 17	·400	RR500247	**PARA-RESIN**·2·C.P. HALL COMPANY
61 NO 28		RR727364	**PARA-SEAL**·8·RED KAP GARMENT COMPANY
69 DE 23		R887339	**PARA-SLAG**·2·METALLURGICAL EXOPRODUCTS, INC
85 JL 16	· 28	R1361281	**PARA TECH**·STRECK LABORATORIES, INC.
		RR208753	**PARA-THOR-MONE**·ELI LILLY & COMPANY
84 NO 27	·629	R1317494	**PARA 12**·STRECK LABORATORIES, INC.
85 JL 30	· 21	R1363824	**PARA 4**·STRECK LABORATORIES, INC.
56 JN 19		RR633864	**PARABAR**·2·ESSO STANDARD OIL COMPANY
66 JL 19		R816027	**PARABIS**·2·DOW CHEMICAL COMPANY
66 OC 04		R830027	**PARABOND**·2·PARA-CHEM, INCORPORATED
82 AP 20	·296	R1228888	**PARABOND**·USM CORPORATION
84 OC 02	· 24	R1308518	**PARAC**·GEORGIA PACIFIC CORPORATION
83 MR 01	· 23	R1239036	**PARACAB II**·PARAGON OPTICAL, INC.
63 MR 26		RR750746	**PARACHEK**·2·HALLIBURTON COMPANY
80 MR 11	· 45	R1141459	**PARACHEM**·PARA-CHEM SOUTHERN, INC.
84 MR 06	27	R1279367	**PARACIDIN**·NAPP CHEMICALS, INC.
51 DE 25	·901	RR556396	**PARACOL**·2·HERCULES POWDER COMPANY
66 AP 19		R810709	**PARADE**·8·ALCO CHEMICAL CO.
58 FE 25		RR661521	**PARADENE**·2·NEVILLE CHEMICAL COMPANY
48 JL 06	· 37	RR502720	**PARADOR**·2·GIVAUDAN-DELAWANNA, INC.
72 JN 27		R942531	**PARADOW**·8·DOW CHEMICAL COMPANY
56 DE 18		RR642224	**PARADYNE**·2·ENJAY COMPANY, INC.
83 MR 01	22	R1239037	**PARAFLEX**·PARAGON OPTICAL, INC.
		RR292295	**PARAFLOW**·STANDARD OIL DEVELOPMENT COMPAN
48 JL 27	·855	RR 46088	**PARAGON**·8·E.W. CONKLIN & SON
61 AU 15		RR723228	**PARAGON**·2·J. M. HUBER CORPORATION
84 JA 10	161	R1354798	**PARAGON**·BECKMAN INSTRUMENTS, INC.
83 MR 01	· 22	R1239036	**PARAGON 18**·PARAGON OPTICAL, INC.
80 MR 11	· 45	R1137131	**PARAGUM**·PARA-CHEM SOUTHERN, INC.
66 MR 22		R809456	**PARAHIB**·2·MILCHEM INCORPORATED
77 MY 03	· 7	R1070049	**PARALAC**·2·TESTWORTH LABORATORIES, INC.
53 JN 09	·323	RR585661	**PARALOID**·2·ROHM & HAAS COMPANY
76 JA 27	·419	R1038076	**PARALOID**·2·ROHM AND HAAS COMPANY
82 JL 27	·461	R1212879	**PARAMAX**·AMERICAN HOSPITAL SUPPLY CORPORAT
50 NO 28	· 79	RR537757	**PARAMEL**·2·ARKANSAS COMPANY, INC.
62 SE 11		RR741166	**PARAMEL**·2·AMERICAN CYANAMID COMPANY
65 FE 02		R788333	**PARAMINE**·2·ARKANSAS CO., INC.
85 MY 28	PEN	SN538617	**PARAMOUNT**·STIRLING MANUFACTURING COMPAN
84 DE 11	·215	R1320253	**PARAMOUNT**·SYVA COMPANY
		RR436288	**PARAMUL**·AMERICAN CYANAMID COMPANY
68 JL 16		R857748	**PARAMUL**·2·AMERICAN CYANAMID COMPANY
65 JA 26		RR788033	**PARAN**·8·DOW CHEMICAL COMPANY
80 MR 11	45	R1137130	**PARANOL**·PARA-CHEM SOUTHERN, INC.
		RR345641	**PARANOX**·STANDARD OIL DEVELOPMENT COMPANY
74 AU 27	·221	R998377	**PARAPAK**·8·EXXON CORPORATION
69 JA 28		R872393	**PARAPERL**·2·CANADIAN HOECHST LIMITED
83 MR 01	23	R1239039	**PARAPERM O2 (BLOCK FORM)**·PARAGON OPTICAL, INC.
63 JN 11		RR759450	**PARAPLAST**·2·REZOLIN, INC.
85 NO 05		SN543136	**PARAPLAST X-TRA**·SHERWOOD MEDICAL COMPAN
48 JN 01	64	RR279547	**PARAPLEX**·8·RESINOUS PRODUCTS & CHEMICAL CO
82 JL 12	151	R1252592	**PARAPLEX**·ROHM AND HAAS COMPANY

69 NO 11		R884834	**PARCRYL**·8·THIBAUT & WALKER CO., INC.
71 OC 28		R926609	**PARCRYL**·8·THIBAUT & WALKER CO., INC.
73 JN 19	·140	R967315	**NU-PAREIL PG**·2·SUCREST CORPORATION
72 NO 21	·184	R957516	**PAREL**·2·HERCULES INCORPORATED
		RR252514	**COMPAGNIE PARENTO C.P.**·D·COMPAGNIE PA
84 JA 10	·175	R1272282	**PAREX**·UOP INC.
		RR411134	**PAREZ**·AMERICAN CYANAMID & CHEMICAL CORPOR
65 JN 01		RR794254	**PAREZ**·2·AMERICAN CYANAMID COMPANY
50 AP 18	·743	RR442798	**PARICIN**·8·BAKER CASTOR OIL COMPANY
56 OC 16		RR639459	**PARID**·2·PETROLITE CORPORATION
81 NO 24	·416	R1189647	**PARIS WALL - BOND**·FORBO NORTH AMERICA, IN
73 JL 17	·153	R989481	**PARK**·D8·RUHR-STICKSTOFF AKTIENGESELLSCHAFT
83 JA 04	· 22	R1232391	**PARK RIDGE**·ESTECH GENERAL CHEMICALS CORPO
85 AU 20	· 24	R1367243	**PARK-STARTS**·GEO. W. PARK SEED CO., INC
50 JN 27	· 29	RR531511	**PARKER PROCESS**·D2·PARKER RUST PROOF COM
50 MY 16	·703	RR529121	**PARKER PROCESSES**·D2·PARKER RUST PROOF C
50 SE 19	·665	RR535608	**A PARKER PRODUCT PARKER RUST PROOF**·D2·PARKER RUST PROOF COMPANY
82 DE 21	·329	R1240749	**PARKER S**·PARKER FERTILIZER COMPANY
63 DE 31		RR766570	**PARKERIZING.**·2·HOOKER CHEMICAL CORPORATIO
74 JL 09	·108	R994470	**PARKERTHANE**·2·PARKER-HANNIFIN CORPORATION
49 JL 12	·430	RR440766	**PARKO**·D2·PARK CHEMICAL COMPANY
84 MR 06	· 33	R1279425	**PARLAY**·IMPERIAL CHEMICAL INDUSTRIES
78 MY 23		R1099902	**NATIONAL ASSOCIATION OF PARLIAMENTARIANS**·NATIONAL ASSOCIATION OF
48 MR 30	·903	RR129685	**PARLODION**·2·E. I. DU PONT DE NEMOURS & COM
48 JA 13	·229	RR500027	**PARLODION**·2·MALLINCKRODT CHEMICAL WORKS
60 DE 27		RR712362	**PARLON**·2·HERCULES POWDER COMPANY
		RR153670	**PARMO**·STANDARD OIL COMPANY, (INCORPORATED
84 NO 13	·229	SN429171	**PAROCRYL**·BASF FARBEN FARBEN AKTIENGSELLSC
48 SE 28	·880	RR355202	**PAROLITE**·2·ROYCE CHEMICAL COMPANY
84 NO 13	·229	R1315235	**PAROSIN**·BASF FARBEN FARBEN AKTIENGESELLSCH
85 AP 23	· 10	SN429173	**PAROTAL**·BASF FARBEN + FARBEN AKTIENGESELL
75 JL 01	· 7	R1020861	**PARQUENCH**·2·PARK CHEMICAL COMPANY
68 JN 25		R856317	**PARR**·2·PARR INSTRUMENT CO.
68 JN 25		R856318	**PARR**·D2·PARR INSTRUMENT CO.
82 JL 20	·315	R1212038	**PARSOL**·GIVAUDAN CORPORATION
		RR 61007	**PARSON'S HOUSEHOLD AMMONIA**·COLUMBIA CHEMICAL WORKS
		RR 60715	**C. C. PARSONS**·COLUMBIA CHEMICAL WORKS
68 FE 20		R848462	**PARSTAR**·2·VWR UNITED CORPORATION
52 SE 16	·805	RR567328	**LIQUID-PART**·2·FREDERIC B. STEVENS, INCORPORA
68 JN 04	· 49	R850396 S	**SURE PART**·8·FREEMAN SUPPLY CO.
72 DE 26	·205	R954800	**COUNT-A-PART**·2·DIAGNOSTIC TECHNOLOGY, INC.
81 SE 22	·502	R1181737	**MY PART**·D·WRI SYSTEMS, INC.
85 OC 29	· 27	SN520810	**PARTAC**·PARTAC PEAT CORPORATION
81 SE 15	·341	R1180734	**PARTICU-LO**·ALLIED CHEMICAL CORPORATION
75 AP 01	· 13	R1013917	**PARTILOK**·2·THICK FILM SYSTEMS, INC.
84 MY 15	·374	R1288552	**PARTINGKOTE**·HEXCEL CORPORATION
77 AU 30	·245	R1077680	**PARTISIL**·2·WHATMAN INC.
85 FE 22	PEN	SN523511	**PARTISPHERE**·WHATMAN INTERNATIONAL LIMITED
85 AU 13	· 29	R1368149	**POOL PARTNERS**·MCNEIL CORPORATION
75 FE 25	·239	R1011777	**THE CORPORATE PARTNERSHIP**·2·ALCO STANDARD CORPORATION
67 NO 07	· 56	RR435134	**PARZATE**·8·E.I. DU PONT DE NEMOURS AND COMP
57 JL 30		RR652867	**PASCO**·2·AMERICAN ART CLAY COMPANY
57 AU 13		RR653644	**PASCO**·2·AMERICAN ART CLAY COMPANY
66 MY 24		R812380	**PASHEA'S**·D8·PRIVATE BRANDS, INC.
68 AP 23		R852134	**EL PASO**·2·EL PASO PRODUCTS COMPANY
80 FE 19	203	R1135856	**ONE-PASS**·ECONOMICS LABORATORY, INC.
84 AP 10	·183	R1283832	**PERMA PASS**·OMI INTERNATIONAL CORPORATION
68 AP 16		R851705	**PROCESSING THE PAST INTO YOUR FUTURE**·2·EL PASO PRODUCTS COMPANY
48 JN 08	·392	RR502181	**PASTALL**·2·HARSHAW CHEMICAL COMPANY
54 SE 14	·248	RR598246	**NOKORODE SOLDERING PASTE**·D2·M. W. DUNTON COMPANY
58 DE 09		RR680245	**BULLDOG LINOLEUM PASTE**·D2·TEMPLAR OIL P
72 NO 14	· 84	R951666	**LIQUI PASTE**·2·ASHLAND OIL, INC.
79 NO 06	· 12	R1129759	**PASTE PLUS**·D·GENERAL TIRE & RUBBER COMPAN
85 MY 16	PEN	SN538085	**PASTE-THE-WALL**·L. E. CARPENTER & COMPANY
78 AU 08	· 72	R1105012	**PASTE THE WALL**·2·ROMAN ADHESIVES, INC.
76 JA 27	·438	R1038306	**INSTITUT PASTEUR**·2·INSTITUT PASTEUR
58 SE 16		RR670464	**PASTURITE**·2·WYANDOTTE CHEMICALS CORPORATI
64 NO 10		R783834	**PASTY PALS**·2·LEPAGE'S, INC.
85 AU 12	PEN	SN552874	**EAGLE STRUCTURAL PATCH**·WILLIAMS BROS.
56 MR 13		RR627569	**PERMA PATCH**·2·MILL CREEK TRANSIT MIX, INC.
61 JL 25		RR722431	**OIL PATCH**·2·HAMMONS PRODUCTS COMPANY
70 AP 21	·169	R889873 S	**EPOXI PATCH**·8·DEXTER CORPORATION
70 SE 22		R903740	**EXO-PATCH**·2·RITE THERM INC.
78 DE 05	· 9	R1113869	**EPOXI-PATCH**·DEXTER CORPORATION
82 JL 13	·169	R1211133	**MAGIC PATCH**·OHIO SEALANTS, INC.
84 JA 24		R1265331 S	**RAPID PATCH**·POLYMER ENGINEERING CORPORAT
77 JA 04	·101	R1051951	**PATCH-A-TATCH**·8·DUNCAN ENTERPRISES
73 NO 13	· 63	R977881	**MAGIC MATCH PATCH STICK**·2·ARTHUR R. DE
81 AP 14	·158	R1159584	**PATCOTE**·C. J. PATTERSON COMPANY
70 JL 21		R893888	**PATEK**·2·AMERACE ESNA CORPORATION
85 JN 10	PEN	SN542037	**PATGEL**·CLOVER MANUFACTURING COMPANY, THE
75 MY 06	· 11	R1029772	**PATH**·2·PARKER LABORATORIES, INC.
84 AP 10	·182	R1283820	**COAG-PATH**·S.E.M.S. SOCIETE D ETUDES ET D EX
60 MY 03		RR701172	**PATH-O-CYTE**·8·PENTEX INCORPORATED
84 NO 20	·432	R1316388	**PATHFINDER (BLOCK FORM)**·KALLESTAD LABO
85 MY 21	· 26	R1351154	**PATHO-GENE**·ENZO BIOCHEM, INC.
85 OC 15	· 40	SN517627	**PATHODX**·DIAGNOSTIC PRODUCTS CORPORATION
84 DE 18	·429	R1321852	**PATHONORM**·NYEGAARD & CO. A/S
66 SE 20		R819701	**PATHOTEC**·2·WARNER-LAMBERT PHARMACEUTICAL
85 JL 30	23	R1363837	**PATHWAY**·BECKMAN INSTRUMENTS, INC
71 MR 23		R912021	**PATINAL**·2·E. MERCK
73 AP 24	265	R963321	**PATINATE**·2·CONVERSION CHEMICAL CORPORATION
76 DE 07	11	R1080178	**PATIONIC**·2·C. J. PATTERSON COMPANY
82 JL 20	315	R1212029	**PATLAC**·C. J. PATTERSON COMPANY

The Compu-Mark Directory of U.S. Trademarks. Vol. 1.1986 ed., p. 63. Reprinted with permission.

APPENDIX C

Instructions for Trademark Applications

Trademark Application Forms:

Trademark/Service Mark Application, Principal Register, with Declaration

Amendment to Allege Use (for intent-to-use applicants)

Statement of Use (for intent-to-use applicants)

Request for Extension of Time (for intent-to-use applicants)

Instructions for Trademark Registration[1]

Filing Requirements

A trademark application consists of (1) a written application form; (2) a drawing of the mark; (3) the required filing fee; and, *only if the application is filed based upon prior use of the mark in commerce*, (4) three specimens showing actual use of the mark on or in connection with the goods or services (see page 24 of this book regarding this last requirement). Each of these elements will be discussed hereafter. The written application is the first of the four forms appended in this section, titled "Trademark/Service Mark Application, Principal Register, with Declaration." [The back page of the form is printed upside down so that it may be affixed to the application file at the top and still be easily read.]

The actual forms included in this appendix may be used to file a trademark application, or photocopies of the forms may be made and submitted.

1. Written Application Form

The application must be written in English. The enclosed form may be used for either a trademark or service mark application. The following explanation covers each blank.

Heading. Identify (a) the mark (for example, "IVORY" or "IVORY and design") and (b) the class number(s) of the goods or services for which registration is sought. The international class number may be obtained from the directory in Appendix A in this book. The class may be left blank if the appropriate class number cannot be determined.

Applicant. The application must be filed in the name of the owner of the mark. Specify, if an individual, applicant's name and citizenship; if a partnership, the names and citizenship of the general partners and the domicile of the partnership; if a corporation or association, the name under which it is incorporated and the state or foreign nation under the laws of which it is organized. Also indicate the applicant's post office address.

Identification of Goods or Services. State briefly the specific goods or services for which the mark is used or intended to be used and for which registration is sought. Use clear and precise language, for example, "men's clothing, namely, belts," or "computer programs for use by lawyers," or "restaurant services."

Basis for Application. The applicant must check at least one of four boxes to specify the basis for filing the application. Usually an application is based upon either (1) prior use of the mark in commerce (first box), or (2) a bona fide intention to use the mark in commerce (the second box), but not both. If both the first and second boxes are checked, the Patent and Trademark Office will *not* accept the application and will return it to the applicant without processing.

The last two boxes pertain to applications filed in the United States pursuant to international agreements, based upon applications or registrations in foreign countries. Applications made on these bases are rare. For additional information regarding foreign-based applications, the applicant may phone the trademark information number [(703) 557-INFO] or contact a private attorney.

If the applicant is using the mark in commerce in relation to all the goods or services listed in the application, check the first box and state each of the following:

---

1   Adapted from "Basic Facts about Trademarks" (Washington, D.C.: U.S. Government Printing Office, 1989).

The date the trademark was first used anywhere in the U.S. on the goods, or in connection with the services, specified in the application;

The date the trademark was first used on the specified goods, or in connection with the specified services, sold or shipped (or rendered) in a type of commerce which may be regulated by Congress;

The type of commerce in which the goods were sold or shipped or services were rendered [for example, "interstate commerce" or "commerce between the United States and (specify foreign country)"]; and

How the mark is used on the goods, or in connection with the services [for example, "the mark is used on labels which are affixed to the goods," or "the mark is used in advertisements for the services"].

If the applicant has a bona fide intention to use the mark in commerce in relation to the goods or services specified in the application, check the second box. This would include situations in which the mark has not been used at all or where the mark has been used on the specified goods or services only within a single state (intrastate commerce).

Execution. The application form must be dated and signed. (See back of form.) The declaration and signature block appear on the back of the form. The Patent and Trademark Office will *not* accept an unsigned application and will return it to the applicant without processing. By signing the form, the applicant is swearing that all the information in the application is believed to be true. If the applicant is an individual, the individual must execute it; if joint applicants, all must execute; if a partnership, one general partner must execute the application; and if a corporation or association, one officer of the organization must execute the application.

2. Drawing

The drawing is a representation of the mark as actually used or intended to be used on the goods or services. There are two types: (a) typed drawings and (b) special form drawings.

All drawings must be made upon pure white durable nonshiny paper 8 1/2 inches wide by 11 inches long. One of the shorter sides of the sheet should be regarded as its top. There must be a margin of at least one inch on the side and bottom of the paper and at least one inch between the drawing of the mark and the heading.

The *drawing* is different than the *specimens*, which are the actual tags or labels (for goods) or advertisements (for services) which evidence use of the mark in commerce. The *drawing* is a black and white, or typed, rendition of the mark which is used in printing the mark in the Official Gazette and on the registration certificate. A copy of the drawing is also filed in the paper records of the Trademark Search Library to provide notice of the pending application.

Heading. Across the top of the drawing, beginning one inch from the top edge and not exceeding one third of the sheet, list on separate lines:

Applicant's name;
Applicant's post office address;
The goods or services specified in the application
 (or typical items of the goods or services if there are many goods or services listed);
Only in an application based on use in commerce—the date of first use of the mark anywhere in the U.S. and the date of first use of the mark in commerce;

Only in an application based on a foreign application—the filing date of the foreign application.

Typed drawing. If the mark is only words, or words and numerals, and the applicant does not wish the registration to be issued for a particular depiction of the words and/or numerals, the mark may be typed in capital letters in the center of the page.

Special form drawing. This form must be used if the applicant wishes the registration for the mark to be issued in a particular style, or if the mark contains a design element. The drawing of the mark must be done in black ink, either with an india ink pen or by a process which will give satisfactory reproduction characteristics. Every line and letter, including words, must be black. This applies to all lines, including lines used for shading. Half-tones and gray are not acceptable. All lines must be clean, sharp, and solid, and not be fine and crowded. A photolithographic reproduction, printer's proof or camera ready copy may be used if otherwise suitable. Photographs are not acceptable. Photocopies are acceptable only if they produce an unusually clear and sharp black and white rendering. The use of white pigment to cover lines is not acceptable.

The preferred size of the drawing of the mark is 2 1/2 inches by 2 1/2 inches, and in no case may be larger than 4 inches by 4 inches. The Patent and Trademark Office will not accept an application with a special form drawing depicted larger than 4 inches by 4 inches and will return the application without processing. If the amount of detail in the mark precludes clear reduction to the required 4 inches by 4 inches size, such detail should not be shown in the drawing but should be verbally described in the body of the application.

Where color is a feature of a mark, the color or colors may be designated in the drawing by the linings shown in the following chart:

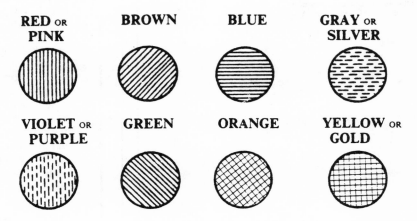

3. Specimens (Examples of Use)

Trademarks may be placed on the goods; on the container for the goods; on displays associated with the goods; on tags or labels attached to the goods; or, if the nature of the goods makes such placement impractical, then on documents associated with the goods or their sale. Service marks may appear in advertisements for the services, or in brochures about the services, or on business cards or stationery used in connection with the services.

For an application based on actual use of the mark in commerce, the applicant must furnish three examples of use, as described in the paragraph above, when the application is filed. The Patent and Trademark Office will not accept an application based on use in commerce without at least one "specimen" and will return it to the applicant without processing.

The three "specimens" may be identical or they may be examples of three different types of uses. The three specimens should be actual labels, tags, containers, displays, etc. for goods; and actual advertisements, brochures, store signs or stationery (if the nature of the services is clear from the letterhead or body of the letter), etc. for services. Specimens may not be larger than 8 1/2 inches by 11 inches and must be capable of being arranged flat. Three-dimensional or bulky material is not acceptable. Photographs or other reproductions clearly and legibly showing the mark on the goods, or on displays associated with the goods, may be submitted if the manner of affixing the mark to the goods, or the nature of the goods, is such that specimens as described above cannot be submitted.

Examples of drawings and specimens

An example is provided below to assist applicants in formatting drawings submitted to the Patent and Trademark Office as part of a trademark or service mark application. Further advice on the submission of specimens, along with several examples, is also included.

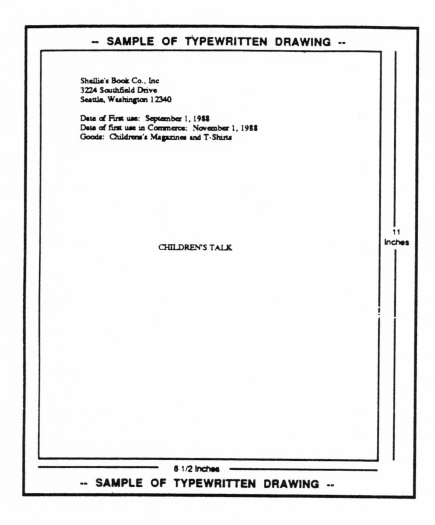

As already, stated, the drawing page must be pure white, durable, non-shiny paper that is 8 1/2 inches wide by 11 inches long. There must be at least a one inch margin on the sides and top of the page between the edge of the page and any information.

The "drawing" on the drawing page in the sample shown at the left is typewritten in all capital letters. Capital letters must be used even if your mark uses capital letters and lower case or all lower case letters. If you wish to have your mark registered in the form in which it is actually used in commerce, you must submit a special form drawing. In that case, the illustration of the mark must be no larger than 4 inches by 4 inches and should be centered on the drawing page. The special form drawing must be black and white. Colors are to be designated by special lining shown above in the "Drawing" section.

Specimens to support use of the above mark on a magazine could consist of the magazine cover and on a T-shirt, labels or tags that are attached or affixed to the goods when they are shipped in commerce. The depiction of labels below is not meant to suggest the form a label must take, only to suggest some possibilities and to distinguish between the nature of a specimen and a drawing. The submitted specimens must be actual samples of how the mark is being used in commerce, that is, actual tags, not a depiction of a tag. If it is impractical to send an actual specimen because of its size, a photograph, clearly showing how the mark is used, may be submitted.

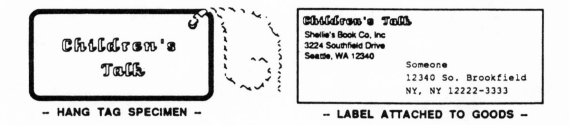

-- HANG TAG SPECIMEN --   -- LABEL ATTACHED TO GOODS --

4. Filing Fee

The fee, effective April 17, 1989, is $175 for each class of goods or services for which the application is made. (See International Classification of Goods and Services in Appendix A.) At least $175 must be submitted for the application to be given a filing date. All payments should be made in United States specie, treasury notes, national bank notes, post office money orders, or certified checks. Personal or business checks may be submitted. Money orders and checks should be made payable to the Commissioner of Patents and Trademarks. Money sent by mail to the Patent and Trademark Office will be at the risk of the sender; letters containing cash should be registered. Remittances made from foreign countries must be payable and immediately negotiable in the United States for the full amount of the fee required. Application fees are non-refundable.

Further Requirements for Intent-to-Use Applicants

An applicant who alleges only a bona fide intention to use a mark in commerce must make use of the mark in commerce before a registration will be issued. After use begins, the applicant must submit, along with specimens evidencing use (see element 3 above) and a fee of $100 per class of goods or services in the application, either (1) an Amendment to Allege Use or (2) a Statement of Use. The difference between these two filings is the timing of the filing. Copies of each of these forms appears in the back of this appendix behind the application form. See the instructions and information concerning the filing of these forms on the back of each form.

Also in the back of this appendix is a form entitled "Request for Extension of Time under 37 CFR 2.89 to File a Statement of Use, with Declaration." This form is intended for use only when an applicant needs to request an extension of time to file a statement of use. See the instructions and information concerning the use of this form on the back of the form.

Communications with the PTO

The application and all other communications should be addressed to The Commissioner of Patents and Trademarks, Washington, D.C. 20231. It is preferred that the applicant indicate his or her or its telephone number on the application form. Once a serial number is assigned to the application, the applicant should refer to this identifying number in all telephone and written communications concerning the application.

Phone Numbers
General Trademark or Patent Information: (703) 557-INFO
Status Information for Particular Trademark Applications: (703) 557-5249
General Copyright Information: (202) 479-0700

TRADEMARK/SERVICE MARK APPLICATION, PRINCIPAL REGISTER, WITH DECLARATION	MARK (Identify the mark)
	CLASS NO. (if known)

TO THE ASSISTANT SECRETARY AND COMMISSIONER OF PATENTS AND TRADEMARKS:

APPLICANT NAME:

APPLICANT BUSINESS ADDRESS:

APPLICANT ENTITY: (Check one and supply requested information)

☐ Individual - Citizenship: (Country) _____

☐ Partnership - Partnership Domicile: (State and Country) _____
Names and Citizenship (Country) of General Partners: _____

_____

☐ Corporation - State (Country, if appropriate) of Incorporation: _____

☐ Other: (Specify Nature of Entity and Domicile) _____

_____

GOODS AND/OR SERVICES:

Applicant requests registration of the above-identified trademark/service mark shown in the accompanying drawing in the United States Patent and Trademark Office on the Principal Register established by the Act of July 5, 1946 (15 U.S.C. 1051 et. seq., as amended.) for the following goods/services: _____

_____

_____

BASIS FOR APPLICATION: (Check one or more, but NOT both the first AND second boxes, and supply requested information)

☐ Applicant is using the mark in commerce on or in connection with the above identified goods/services. (15 U.S.C. 1051(a), as amended.) Three specimens showing the mark as used in commerce are submitted with this application.
• Date of first use of the mark anywhere: _____
• Date of first use of the mark in commerce which the U.S. Congress may regulate:_____
• Specify the type of commerce: _____
                  (e.g., interstate, between the U.S. and a specified foreign country)
• Specify manner or mode of use of mark on or in connection with the goods/services:_____

_____
      (e.g., trademark is applied to labels, service mark is used in advertisements)

☐ Applicant has a bona fide intention to use the mark in commerce on or in connection with the above identified goods/services. (15 U.S.C. 1051(b), as amended.)
• Specify intended manner or mode of use of mark on or in connection with the goods/services:_____

_____
      (e.g., trademark will be applied to labels, service mark will be used in advertisements)

☐ Applicant has a bona fide intention to use the mark in commerce on or in connection with the above identified goods/services, and asserts a claim of priority based upon a foreign application in accordance with 15 U.S.C. 1126(d), as amended.
• Country of foreign filing: _____ • Date of foreign filing: _____

☐ Applicant has a bona fide intention to use the mark in commerce on or in connection with the above identified goods/services and, accompanying this application, submits a certification or certified copy of a foreign registration in accordance with 15 U.S.C. 1126(e), as amended.
• Country of registration:_____ • Registration number: _____

Note: Declaration, on Reverse Side, MUST be Signed

DECLARATION

The undersigned being hereby warned that willful false statements and the like so made are punishable by fine or imprisonment, or both, under 18 U.S.C. 1001, and that such willful false statements may jeopardize the validity of the application or any resulting registration, declares that he/she is properly authorized to execute this application on behalf of the applicant; he/she believes the applicant to be the owner of the trademark/service mark sought to be registered, or, if the application is being filed under 15 U.S.C. 1051(b), he/she believes applicant to be entitled to use such mark in commerce; to the best of his/her knowledge and belief no other person, firm, corporation, or association has the right to use the above identified mark in commerce, either in the identical form thereof or in such near resemblance thereto as to be likely, when used on or in connection with the goods/services of such other person, to cause confusion, or to cause mistake, or to deceive; and that all statements made of his/her own knowledge are true and all statements made on information and belief are believed to be true.

Date	Signature
Telephone Number	Print or Type Name and Position

INSTRUCTIONS AND INFORMATION FOR APPLICANT

To receive a filing date, the application must be completed and signed by the applicant and submitted along with:

1. The prescribed fee for each class of goods/services listed in the application;
2. A drawing of the mark in conformance with 37 CFR 2.52;
3. If the application is based on use of the mark in commerce, three (3) specimens (evidence) of the mark as used in commerce for each class of goods/services listed in the application. All three specimens may be the same and may be in the nature of: (a) labels showing the mark which are placed on the goods; (b) a photograph of the mark as it appears on the goods, (c) brochures or advertisements showing the mark as used in connection with the services.

Verification of the application - The application must be signed in order for the application to receive a filing date. Only the following person may sign the verification (Declaration) for the application, depending on the applicant's legal entity: (1) the individual applicant; (b) an officer of the corporate applicant; (c) one general partner of a partnership applicant; (d) all joint applicants.

Additional information concerning the requirements for filing an application are available in a booklet entitled Basic Facts about Trademarks, which may be obtained by writing:

U.S. DEPARTMENT OF COMMERCE
Patent and Trademark Office
Washington, D.C. 20231

Or by calling: (703) 557-INFO

This form is estimated to take 15 minutes to complete. Time will vary depending upon the needs of the individual case. Any comments on the amount of time you require to complete this form should be sent to the Office of Management and Organization, U.S. Patent and Trademark Office, Washington D.C. 20231, and to the Office of Information and Regulatory Affairs, Office of Management and Budget, Washington, D.C. 20503.

<table>
<tr><td>AMENDMENT TO ALLEGE USE
UNDER 37 CFR 2.76, WITH
DECLARATION</td><td>MARK (Identify the mark)</td></tr>
<tr><td></td><td>SERIAL NO.</td></tr>
</table>

TO THE ASSISTANT SECRETARY AND COMMISSIONER OF PATENTS AND TRADEMARKS:

APPLICANT NAME:

Applicant requests registration of the above-identified trademark/service mark in the United States Patent and Trademark Office on the Principal Register established by the Act of July 5, 1946 (15 U.S.C. 1051 et. seq., as amended). Three specimens showing the mark as used in commerce are submitted with this amendment.

☐   Check here if Request to Divide under 37 CFR 2.87 is being submitted with this amendment.

Applicant is using the mark in commerce on or in connection with the following goods/services:

_____

_____

(NOTE: Goods/services listed above may not be broader than the goods/services identified in the application as filed)

Date of first use of mark anywhere: _____

Date of first use of mark in commerce
which the U.S. Congress may regulate: _____

Specify type of commerce: (e.g., interstate, between the U.S. and a specified foreign country) _____

_____

Specify manner or mode of use of mark on or in connection with the goods/services: (e.g., trademark is applied to labels, service mark is used in advertisements) _____

_____

The undersigned being hereby warned that willful false statements and the like so made are punishable by fine or imprisonment, or both, under 18 U.S.C. 1001, and that such willful false statements may jeopardize the validity of the application or any resulting registration, declares that he/she is properly authorized to execute this Amendment to Allege Use on behalf of the applicant; he/she believes the applicant to be the owner of the trademark/service mark sought to be registered; the trademark/ service mark is now in use in commerce; and all statements made of his/her own knowledge are true and all statements made on information and belief are believed to be true.

_____   _____
Date   Signature

_____   _____
Telephone Number   Print or Type Name and Position

INSTRUCTIONS AND INFORMATION FOR APPLICANT

In an application based upon a bona fide intention to use a mark in commerce, applicant must use its mark in commerce before a registration will be issued. After use begins, the applicant must submit, along with evidence of use (specimens) and the prescribed fee(s), **either:**

(1) an Amendment to Allege Use under 37 CFR 2.76, or

(2) a Statement of Use under 37 CFR 2.88.

The difference between these two filings is the timing of the filing. Applicant may file an Amendment to Allege Use before approval of the mark for publication for opposition in the **Official Gazette**, or, if a final refusal has been issued, prior to the expiration of the six month response period. Otherwise, applicant must file a Statement of Use after the Office issues a Notice of Allowance. The Notice of Allowance will issue after the opposition period is completed if no successful opposition is filed. Neither Amendment to Allege Use or Statement of Use papers will be accepted by the Office during the period of time between approval of the mark for publication for opposition in the **Official Gazette** and the issuance of the Notice of Allowance.

Applicant may call (703) 557-5249 to determine whether the mark has been approved for publication for opposition in the **Official Gazette.**

Before filing an Amendment to Allege Use or a Statement of Use, applicant must use the mark in commerce on or in connection with **all** of the goods/services for which applicant will seek registration, **unless** applicant submits with the papers, a request to divide out from the application the goods or services to which the Amendment to Allege Use or Statement of Use pertains. (See: 37 CFR 2.87, Dividing an application)

Applicant **must** submit with an Amendment to Allege Use or a Statement of Use:

(1) the appropriate fee of $100 per class of goods/services listed in the Amendment to Allege Use or the Statement of Use, and

(2) three (3) specimens or facsimiles of the mark as used in commerce for each class of goods/services asserted (e.g., photograph of mark as it appears on goods, label containing mark which is placed on goods, or brochure or advertisement showing mark as used in connection with services).

Cautions/Notes concerning completion of this Amendment to Allege Use form:

(1) The goods/services identified in the Amendment to Allege Use must be within the scope of the goods/services identified in the application as filed. Applicant may delete goods/services. Deleted goods/services may not be reinstated in the application at a later time.

(2) Applicant may list dates of use for only one item in each class of goods/services identified in the Amendment to Allege Use. However, applicant must have used the mark in commerce on all the goods/services in the class. Applicant must identify the particular item to which the dates apply.

(3) Only the following person may sign the verification of the Amendment to Allege Use, depending on the applicant's legal entity: (a) the individual applicant; (b) an officer of corporate applicant; (c) one general partner of partnership applicant; (d) all joint applicants.

<table>
<tr><td rowspan="2">STATEMENT OF USE
UNDER 37 CFR 2.88, WITH
DECLARATION</td><td>MARK (Identify the mark)</td></tr>
<tr><td>SERIAL NO.</td></tr>
</table>

TO THE ASSISTANT SECRETARY AND COMMISSIONER OF PATENTS AND TRADEMARKS:

APPLICANT NAME:

NOTICE OF ALLOWANCE ISSUE DATE:

Applicant requests registration of the above-identified trademark/service mark in the United States Patent and Trademark Office on the Principal Register established by the Act of July 5, 1946 (15 U.S.C. 1051 et. seq., as amended). Three (3) specimens showing the mark as used in commerce are submitted with this statement.

☐ Check here only if a Request to Divide under 37 CFR 2.87 is being submitted with this Statement.

Applicant is using the mark in commerce on or in connection with the following goods/services: (Check One)

☐ Those goods/services identified in the Notice of Allowance in this application.

☐ Those goods/services identified in the Notice of Allowance in this application except: (Identify goods/services to be deleted from application) _____

_____

_____

Date of first use of mark anywhere: _____

Date of first use of mark in commerce which the U.S. Congress may regulate: _____

Specify type of commerce: (e.g., interstate, between the U.S. and a specified foreign country) _____

_____

Specify manner or mode of use of mark on or in connection with the goods/services: (e.g., trademark is applied to labels, service mark is used in advertisements) _____

_____

The undersigned being hereby warned that willful false statements and the like so made are punishable by fine or imprisonment, or both, under 18 U.S.C. 1001, and that such willful false statements may jeopardize the validity of the application or any resulting registration, declares that he/she is properly authorized to execute this Statement of Use on behalf of the applicant; he/she believes the applicant to be the owner of the trademark/service mark sought to be registered; the trademark/ service mark is now in use in commerce; and all statements made of his/her own knowledge are true and all statements made on information and belief are believed to be true.

_____
Date

_____
Signature

_____
Telephone Number

_____
Print or Type Name and Position

PTO Form 1580 (REV. 9/89)
OMB No. 06510023
Exp. 6-30-92

U.S. DEPARTMENT OF COMMERCE/Patent and Trademark Office

INSTRUCTIONS AND INFORMATION FOR APPLICANT

In an application based upon a bona fide intention to use a mark in commerce, applicant must use its mark in commerce before a registration will be issued. After use begins, the applicant must submit, along with evidence of use (specimens) and the prescribed fee(s), either:

(1) an Amendment to Allege Use under 37 CFR 2.76, or
(2) a Statement of Use under 37 CFR 2.88.

The difference between these two filings is the timing of the filing. Applicant may file an Amendment to Allege Use before approval of the mark for publication for opposition in the **Official Gazette**, or, if a final refusal has been issued, prior to the expiration of the six month response period. Otherwise, applicant must file a Statement of Use after the Office issues a Notice of Allowance. The Notice of Allowance will issue after the opposition period is completed if no successful opposition is filed. Neither Amendment to Allege Use or Statement of Use papers will be accepted by the Office during the period of time between approval of the mark for publication for opposition in the **Official Gazette** and the issuance of the Notice of Allowance.

Applicant may call (703) 557-5249 to determine whether the mark has been approved for publication for opposition in the **Official Gazette.**

Before filing an Amendment to Allege Use or a Statement of Use, applicant must use the mark in commerce on or in connection with **all** of the goods/services for which applicant will seek registration, **unless** applicant submits with the papers, a request to divide out from the application the goods or services to which the Amendment to Allege Use or Statement of Use pertains. (See: 37 CFR 2.87, Dividing an application)

Applicant **must** submit with an Amendment to Allege Use or a Statement of Use:

(1) the appropriate fee of $100 per class of goods/services listed in the Amendment to Allege Use or the Statement of Use, and

(2) three (3) specimens or facsimiles of the mark as used in commerce for each class of goods/services asserted (e.g., photograph of mark as it appears on goods, label containing mark which is placed on goods, or brochure or advertisement showing mark as used in connection with services).

Cautions/Notes concerning completion of this Statement of Use form:

(1) The goods/services identified in the Statement of Use must be identical to the goods/services identified in the Notice of Allowance. Applicant may delete goods/services. Deleted goods/services may not be reinstated in the application at a later time.

(2) Applicant may list dates of use for only one item in each class of goods/services identified in the Statement of Use. However, applicant must have used the mark in commerce on all the goods/services in the class. Applicant must identify the particular item to which the dates apply.

(3) Only the following person may sign the verification of the Statement of Use, depending on the applicant's legal entity: (a) the individual applicant; (b) an officer of corporate applicant; (c) one general partner of partnership applicant; (d) all joint applicants.

REQUEST FOR EXTENSION OF TIME UNDER 37 CFR 2.89 TO FILE A STATEMENT OF USE, WITH DECLARATION	MARK (Identify the mark)
	SERIAL NO.

TO THE ASSISTANT SECRETARY AND COMMISSIONER OF PATENTS AND TRADEMARKS:

APPLICANT NAME:

NOTICE OF ALLOWANCE MAILING DATE:

Applicant requests a six-month extension of time to file the Statement of Use under 37 CFR 2.88 in this application.

☐ Check here if a Request to Divide under 37 CFR 2.87 is being submitted with this request.

Applicant has a continued bona fide intention to use the mark in commerce in connection with the following goods/services: (Check one below)

☐ Those goods/services identified in the Notice of Allowance in this application.

☐ Those goods/services identified in the Notice of Allowance in this application except: (Identify goods/services to be **deleted** from application) _____

_____

This is the _____ request for an Extension of Time following mailing of the Notice of Allowance.
(Specify first - fifth)

If this is not the first request for an Extension of Time, check one box below. If the first box is checked, explain the circumstance(s) of the non-use in the space provided:

☐ Applicant has not used the mark in commerce yet on all goods/services specified in the Notice of Allowance; however, applicant has made the following ongoing efforts to use the mark in commerce on or in connection with each of the goods/services specified above:

_____

_____

If additional space is needed, please attach a separate sheet to this form

☐ Applicant believes that it has made valid use of the mark in commerce, as evidenced by the Statement of Use submitted with this request; however, if the Statement of Use is found by the Patent and Trademark Office to be fatally defective, applicant will need additional time in which to file a new statement.

The undersigned being hereby warned that willful false statements and the like so made are punishable by fine or imprisonment, or both, under 18 U.S.C. 1001, and that such willful false statements may jeopardize the validity of the application or any resulting registration, declares that he/she is properly authorized to execute this Request for Extension of Time to File a Statement of Use on behalf of the applicant; he/she believes the applicant to be the owner of the trademark/service mark sought to be registered; and all statements made of his/her own knowledge are true and all statements made on information and belief are believed to be true.

_____
Date

_____
Signature

_____
Telephone Number

_____
Print or Type Name and Position

PTO Form 1581 (REV. 9/89)
OMB No. 06510023
Exp. 6-30-92

U.S. DEPARTMENT OF COMMERCE/Patent and Trademark Office

INSTRUCTIONS AND INFORMATION FOR APPLICANT

Applicant must file a Statement of Use within six months after the mailing of the Notice of Allowance in an application based upon a bona fide intention to use a mark in commerce, UNLESS, within that same period, applicant submits a request for a six-month extension of time to file the Statement of Use. The request **must**:

(1) be in writing,
(2) include applicant's verified statement of continued bona fide intention to use the mark in commerce,
(3) specify the goods/services to which the request pertains as they are identified in the Notice of Allowance, and
(4) include a fee of $100 for each class of goods/services.

Applicant may request four further six-month extensions of time. No extension may extend beyond 36 months from the issue date of the Notice of Allowance. Each request must be filed within the previously granted six-month extension period and must include, in addition to the above requirements, a showing of **GOOD CAUSE**. This good cause showing must include:

(1) applicant's statement that the mark has not been used in commerce yet on all the goods or services specified in the Notice of Allowance with which applicant has a continued bona fide intention to use the mark in commerce, **and**

(2) applicant's statement of ongoing efforts to make such use, which may include the following: (a) product or service research or development, (b) market research, (c) promotional activities, (d) steps to acquire distributors, (e) steps to obtain required governmental approval, or (f) similar specified activity .

Applicant may submit one additional six-month extension request during the existing period in which applicant files the Statement of Use, unless the granting of this request would extend beyond 36 months from the issue date of the Notice of Allowance. As a showing of good cause, applicant should state its belief that applicant has made valid use of the mark in commerce, as evidenced by the submitted Statement of Use, but that if the Statement is found by the PTO to be defective, applicant will need additional time in which to file a new statement of use.

Only the following person may sign the verification of the Request for Extentsion of Time, depending on the applicant's legal entity: (a) the individual applicant; (b) an officer of corporate applicant; (c) one general partner of partnership applicant; (d) all joint applicants.

✿ U.S.GOVERNMENT PRINTING OFFICE:1989-261-920-00075

Bibliography

For further reading and reference

AA sponsors logo, packaging study. (1987). *Advertising Age*, May 11, 56.

Alexander, J. (1989). What's in a name? Too much, said the FCC. *Sales and Marketing Management*, January, 75-76+.

Atlanta card firm faces getting aced by Trump. (1989). *Jet*, July 31, 23.

Ballard, Lee. (1986). What's in a name? *Dallas Magazine*, January, 195-97.

Barach, Arnold. (1971). *Famous American Trademarks*. Washington, D.C.: Public Affairs Press.

Baron, Dennis. (1990). *Declining Grammar*. Urbana, Illinois: National Council of Teachers of English.

Basic facts about trademarks. (1990). Washington, D.C.: U.S. Government Printing Office.

The Basis of brand valuation. (1989). *Accountancy*, March, 32.

Beer brand names—US and Canada. (1987-88). *Beverage world*, Databank issue, 389-90.

Bekey, Michelle. (1984). Naming your company. *Working Woman*, April, 124-25.

Belkin, L. (1987). The prisoner of Seventh Avenue: how Halston lost the right to his own name. *New York Times Magazine*, March 15, 16-22+.

Bermar, Amy, Berown, Lauren, and Lyons, Dan. (1988). Nice firm—sorry about the name. *PC Week*, July 4, 127.

Berry, Leonard L., Lefkowith, Edwin F., and Clark, Terry. (1988). In services, what's in a name? *Harvard Business Review*, September-October, 28-30.

Bogus blues. (1980). *Time*, November 24, 92.

Borchard, W.M. (1985). Corporate name search recommended. *Advertising Age*, July 8, 40.

Borchard, W.M. (1986). Courts penalize trademark misdeeds. *Advertising Age*, January 6, 34.

Borchard, W.M., Chairman. (1986). *Current developments in trademark law.* Prepared for distribution at the Current Developments in Trademark Law Program, July 17-18, 1986, New York City.

Borchard, W.M. (1985). Delay can bar trademark infringement remedy. *Advertising Age*, May 6, 48.

Borchard, W. M. (1986). Judge takes a functional look at trademarks. *Advertising Age*, April 21, 52.

Brand name policy boosts assets. (1988). *Accountancy*, October, 38-39.

Brand names must be managed like financial assets. (1987). *Marketing News*, November 6, 31.

Brands and Their Companies. (1990). Detroit: Gale Research.

Bronson, Gail. (1985). As companies gamble on creating new images. *U.S. News & World Report*, September 16, 76-77.

Brown, Paul B. (1988). License to steal. *Inc.*, December, 141-42.

Brown, Paul B. and Mangelsdorf, Martha E. (1987). Tex's Chain Saw Manicure. *Inc.,* November, 130-33.

Burgunder, L.B. (1985). An economic approach to trademark genericism. *American Business Law Journal*, Fall, 391-416.

Campbell, B. (1986). Rechristening the company. *Working Woman*, September, 34-35.

Carls, K. (1989). Corporate coats of arms. *Harvard Business Review*, May-June, 135-39.

Chajet, Clive. (1984). What does your firm's name say to customers? *Nation's Business*, June, 38R-39R.

Charmasson, Henri. (1988). *The Name Is the Game: How to Name a Company or Product.* Homewood, Illinois: Dow Jones-Irwin.

Clark, V. (1988). Identify yourself. *Canadian Business*, January, 21-22.

Coleman, M. (1987). Thomas Dolby settles suit over name. *Rolling Stone*, May 7, 10.

Competitiveness, anyone? (1987). *The New Republic*, March 16, 12.

The Compu-Mark Directory of U.S. Trademarks. (1986). Washington, D.C.: Compu-Mark Company.

Cook, Alison. (1987). What's in a name: for Lee Ballard, life is trying to prove that a rose by any other name wouldn't smell as sweet. *Texas Monthly*, August, 130-31.

Cook, D. and others. (1986). Goodyear tries to deflate a rival blimp. *Business Week*, January 20, 30.

Court date set for ruling on McSleep motel chain. (1988). *Restaurant Business*, January 20, 28.

Crain, R. (1985). New logo will solve P&G rumor trouble. *Advertising Age*, May 9, 50.

Diamond, Sidney. (1981). *Trademark Problems and How to Avoid Them*. Chicago: Crain Books.

Directories in Print. (1990). Detroit: Gale Research.

Dunphy, J.F. and Agnew, B.A. (1988). A push for trademark reform. *Chemical Week*, May 18, 9+.

Dun's Electronic Yellow Pages. (1990). Parsippany, N.J.: Dun's Marketing Services.

Edwards, Sarah and Edwards, Paul. (1989). Naming your company. *Home office computing*, July, 28.

Ellis-Simons, P. Picking an image. (1986). *Venture*, February, 30.

Everyone's Guide to Copyrights, Trademarks, and Patents. (1990). Philadelphia: Running Press.

A feeling for the market. (1987). *The Economist*, February 28, 82-83.

Fisher, K. L. (1989). All in a name. *Forbes*, March 6, 166.

Fleischer, L. (1985). Perils of a parodist. *Publishers Weekly*, November 1, 69.

Freeman, L. (1985). After devil of fight, P&G gives up: famed logo off products. *Advertising Age*, April 29, 3+.

Hungry tigers need bright stripes to survive in the corporate jungle. (1985). *Marketing News*, December 20, 4.

Illinois Certified List. (1990). Springfield: Secretary of State.

Index to Trademark and Service Classes. (1990). Washington, D.C.: United States Patent and Trademark Office.

Index to Trademarks Registered with the U.S. Patent and Trademark Office. (1990). Washington, D.C.: United States Patent and Trademark Office.

Is it real? Counterfeit goods are a big business—how to avoid getting ripped off. (1987). *Glamour*, May, 210.

Jordan, Nick. (1983). Picking a name for the corporate child. *Psychology Today*, October, 72.

Kanner, Bernice. (1983). The game of the name: corporate-identity changes. *New York*, August 29, 28-30.

Kanner, Bernice. (1987). The new name game. *New York*, March 16, 16-17.

Kiley, D. (1987). McDonald's bares teeth over prefix: fast-food firm fights for exclusive right to Mc. *AdWeek Marketing Week*, October 26, 2.

Knowing when to redesign is critical. (1988). *Marketing News*, March 14, 48.

Kovach, Jeffrey L. (1985). Corporate identity; programs shed arty image, stress unification. *Industry Week*, August 19, 21-22.

Lindley, David. (1987). What's in a McName? *Mother Jones*, January, 15-16.

McCarthy, J. Thomas. (1984). *Trademarks and Unfair Competition.* Rochester, N.Y.: The Lawyers Co-operative Publishing Co.

Mamis, Robert A. (1984). Name-calling: what the name of your company and products say about you and your business. *Inc.*, July, 67-72.

Masten, D.L. Logo's power depends on how well it communicates with target market. (1988). *Marketing News*, December 5, 20.

Meyerowitz, S.A. (1988). This column's for you! Choosing and protecting slogans. *Business Marketing*, June, 13-15.

Million Dollar Directory. (1990). Parsnippany, N.J.: Dun's Marketing Services.

Murphy, John and Rowe, Michael. (1988). *How to Design Trade Marks and Logos.* Cincinnati: North Light Books.

The name game. (1986). *Newsweek*, January 20, 46.

Name game. (1981). *Time*, August 31, 41-42.

The name's the game. (1988). *Economist*, December 24, 100.

Oathout, John D. (1981). *Trademarks*. New York: Charles Scribner.

The Official Gazette. (1990). Washington, D.C.: United States Patent and Trademark Office.

Petock, Michael F. (1984). *Patents, Trademarks, Copyrights and Trade Secrets*. N.Pl.: N. Pub.

Quarembo, C. (1985). Trademarking your name. *Venture*, June, 34.

Quinn, Hal. (1987). Ceasing and desisting. *Maclean's*, December 7, 61.

Revlon must change package similar to Soft Sheen's. (1987). *Jet*, October 19, 18.

Room, Adrian. (1982). *Dictionary of Trade Name Origins*. London: Routledge & Regan Paul.

Rudolph, B. (1986). The pros who play the name game. *Time*, November 3, 63.

Samuels, Jeffrey M., ed. (1987). *Patent, trademark, and copyright laws*. Washington, D.C.: The Bureau of National Affairs.

Schwartz, John. (1987). What really is in a name? Big bucks, for the growing 'naming' industry. *Newsweek*, November 30, 55.

Seidel, Arthur H. (1986). *What the General Practitioner Should Know About Trademarks and Copyrights*. Philadelphia: American Law Institute-American Bar Association Committee on Continuing Professional Education.

Shepard's U.S. Patents and Trademarks Citations. (1990). New York: McGraw-Hill.

Siegel, L.B. (1989). Planning for a life-long logo. *Marketing Communications*, March, 44-46+.

Smedley, P. (1988). How new name, logo, boosted gasoline, C-store business. *National Petroleum News*, December, 42-44.

Soft drink/bottled water brand names. (1987-88). *Beverage World*, Databank issue, 391-92.

Spadoni, M. (1985). Harley-Davidson revs up to improve image. *Advertising Age*, August 5, 30.

Standard and Poor's Register of Corporations. (1990). New York: Standard and Poor's Corporation.

State Trademark and Unfair Competition Law. (1989). New York: United States Trademark Association.

Sued by McDonald's, a Santa Cruz eatery refuses to cowtow. (1988). *People Weekly*, May 2, 81.

Thomas, David. (1981). The game of the name is forget it. *Maclean's*, January 19, 27.

Thomas Register of American Manufacturers. (1990). New York: Thomas Publishing Company.

The Trademark Register of the United States. (1990). Washington, D.C.: Patent Searching Service.

Trademark update: a roundup of news and tips on the proper use of trademark. (1989). *Writer's Digest*, June, 45-46.

TRADEMARKSCAN. (1990). North Quincy, Ma.: Thomson & Thomson.

TRINET. (1990). Parsnippany, N.J.: Trinet Company.

Unikel, A.L. (1987). Imitation might be flattering, but beware of trademark infringement. *Marketing News*, September 11, 20.

Valuing brands. what's in a name? (1988). *Economist*, August 27, 62-63.

Verespej, Michael A. (1987). Why non-name names? *Industry Week*, August 10, 21.

What's in a name? (1987). *Fortune*, September 14, 6.

Whitcomb, Paulette. (1988) What's in a name? *Colorado Business Magazine*, August, 45-46.

Wingo, Walter S. (1982). Why companies keep changing their names. *U.S. News & World Report*, July 12, 73.

Zinkhan, G.M. and Martin, C.R., Jr. (1987). New brand names and inferential beliefs: some insights on naming new products. *Journal of Business Research*, April, 157-72.

Index

THE BLACK BEAUTY CORPORATE KIT
(See Order Blank on Next Page)

The Black Beauty Corporate Outfit

By special arrangement with Julius Blumberg, Inc., The P. Gaines Co. will provide a complete corporate kit with the following outstanding features:

1. A three-ring Corporate Record Book with 24K gold trim and lustrous black vinyl slip case. Corporate name is printed on a gold label and inserted into acetate label holder. Record Book includes a Stock Transfer Ledger of 8 pages, bound in a separate section, Mylar-coated Index Tabs, with five important divisions, 50 blank sheets of rag content 20-lb. bond Minute Paper, and exclusive Corporate Record Tickler.

2. A Corporate Seal stored inside the Corporate Record Book in a zipper pouch, 1 5/8" diameter, custom finished with corporate name, state, and year. Long corporate names (over 45 characters and spaces) require a 2" diameter seal, at an extra charge of $7.00.

3. 20 custom printed and numbered Stock Certificates with full page numbered stubs. Each certificate is custom printed with corporate name, state, and officers' titles.

ORDER FORM—Remit with payment to The P. Gaines Co., Box 2253, Oak Park, IL 60303

For all corporate kit orders, please type or print the following information:

Corporate name exactly as on certificate of incorporation..

State of incorporation..

Year of incorporation..

Officers who will sign share certificates (President and Secretary-Treasurer will be listed unless specified otherwise)..

Basic price of corporate kit	<u>$55.95</u>
For long corporate names	
(over 45 characters and spaces), add an additional $7.00	_.__
7% Illinois sales tax (Illinois residents only)	3.92
Shipping by UPS (delivery within 3 weeks from receipt of your order) OK	<u>4.00</u>
*Shipping by air express (delivery within 4 days from receipt of your order)	<u>25.00</u>
TOTAL	

Ship to:

Your name..Address...
                                        (Street address required)
City..State...Zip....................

*4-day RUSH orders must be paid for either by Certified Check or Money Order.

FIVE EASY STEPS TO SETTING UP AN IRS-APPROVED RETIREMENT PLAN FOR YOUR SMALL BUSINESS

The Small Business Retirement Dilemma

Less than 20 percent of small businesses in this country currently have retirement plans for their employees. As a result, businesses with 25 or fewer employees cover an average of only one in seven workers with company pension plans.

The Solution

Thanks to new federal pension laws, almost any business that is profitable enough to pay its employee(s) a salary can now start a retirement plan immediately, as explained in *Five Easy Steps to Setting Up an IRS-Approved Retirement Plan*. The author shows the advantages of Simplified Employee Pensions (SEPs) for most small businesses and walks the reader step-by-step through the process of setting up and maintaining an SEP.

With this type of qualified pension plan, you can:

- choose a retirement arrangement that is either employer financed, employee financed, or a combination of each
- prepare for a more secure future, whether you are self-employed (a sole proprietor), a partner, or a corporate owner-employee
- contribute up to a maximum of $30,000 a year per employee to the retirement fund
- take tax-free benefits out of an incorporated business
- offer a powerful incentive for hiring and keeping your most qualified and valuable employees
- have the option of making contributions in profitable years or skipping pension set-asides in lean years

Many small businesses do not have retirement funds because of poor planning, a lack of awareness or a lack of information about the subject, not because of a lack of money. Since virtually any business that is profitable enough to pay its employee(s) a salary can now start a pension fund under the new law, no small business owner can afford any longer to jeopardize his and his employees' future by neglecting retirement planning. This book includes all needed forms and information about SEPs. It will show you the simple procedure to open your own business pension plan, which, with regular contributions, can grow to almost unbelievable size.

ISBN 0-936284-33-1 $14.95